The Christmas Hirelings

THE CHRISTMAS HIRELINGS

THE
CHRISTMAS
HIRELINGS

✳

BY

M. E. BRADDON

ILLUSTRATED BY F. H. TOWNSEND

LONDON
SIMPKIN, MARSHALL, HAMILTON, KENT & CO.
LIMITED
STATIONERS' HALL COURT
1894

LONDON :
PRINTED BY WILLIAM CLOWES AND SONS, LIMITED,
STAMFORD STREET AND CHARING CROSS.

PREFACE.

I HAD long wished to write a story about children, which should be interesting to childish readers, and yet not without interest for grown-up people: but that desire might never have been realized without the unexpected impulse of a suggestion, dropped casually in the freedom of conversation at a table where the clever hostess is ever an incentive to bright thoughts. The talk was of Christmas; and almost everybody agreed that the season, considered from the old-fashioned festal standpoint, was pure irony. Was it not a time of extra burdens, of manifold claims upon everybody's purse and care, of great expectations from all sorts of people, of worry and weariness? Except for the children! There we were unanimous.

Christmas was the children's festival—for us a rush and a scramble, and a perpetual paying away of money ; for them a glimpse of Fairyland.

"If we had no children of our own," said my left-hand neighbour, "we ought to hire some for Christmas."

I thought it was a pretty fancy ; and on that foundation built the little story of the Christmas Hirelings, which is now reproduced in book form from last year's Christmas Number of the *Lady's Pictorial,* and which I hope even after that wide circulation all over the English-speaking world may find a new public at home— the public of mothers and aunts and kind uncles, in quest of stories that please children. This story was a labour of love, a holiday task, written beside the fire in the long autumn evenings when the south-west wind was howling in the Forest trees outside.

The living models for the three children were close at hand, dear and familiar to the writer ; and Moppet's long words and quaint little mannerisms are but the pale reproduction of words and looks and gestures in the tiny girl who was then my next-door neighbour, and who is now far away in the shadow of the Himalayas.

The character of Mr. Danby, whom some of my critics have been kind enough to praise, was suggested by the following passage in the first series of the "Greville Memoirs," copied in my commonplace-book long ago, when everybody was reading those delightful reminiscences :—

"Old Creevy—an attorney or barrister—married a widow, who died a few years ago. She had something, he nothing. His wife died, upon which event he was thrown upon the world with about two hundred a year, or less, no home, few connections, a great many acquaintance, a good constitution, and extraordinary spirits. He possesses nothing but his clothes, no property of any sort; he leads a vagrant life, visiting a number of people who are delighted to have him, and sometimes roving about to various places as fancy happens to direct, and staying till he has spent what money he has in his pocket. He has no servant, no home, no creditors; he buys everything as he wants it at the place he is at;

he has no ties upon him, and has his time entirely at his own disposal and that of his friends. He is certainly a living proof that a man may be perfectly happy and exceedingly poor, or rather without riches, for he suffers none of the privations of poverty, and enjoys many of the advantages of wealth. I think he is the only man I know in society who possesses nothing."

M. E. B.

Lyndhurst,
  November 1st, 1894.

LIST OF ILLUSTRATIONS.

THE CHRISTMAS HIRELINGS

THE CHRISTMAS HIRELINGS.

PROLOGUE.

HE scene was the library at Penlyon Place, commonly called for shortness—Place. The personages were Sir John Penlyon, a great landed proprietor, and a fine gentleman of the early Victorian school; his niece, Miss Adela Hawberk, a smart young lady, whose paternal home was in South Kensington; and Mr. Danby, the useful friend, whose home was everywhere. Home of his own Mr. Danby had none. He had drifted lightly on the stream of life for the last forty years, living in other people's houses, and, more or less, at other people's expense; yet there lived not the man or woman who would have dared to describe Mr. Danby as a sponge or a toady, as anybody's hanger-on or parasite. Mr. Danby only went where he was wanted; and the graces of his manner and the qualities of his mind and heart were such that Mr. Danby was wanted everywhere. He had invitations three years deep. His engagements were as far in the future as the calculations in the nautical almanac. Some people, who had been trying for years to get Mr. Danby to their houses, compared him to that star whose inhabitants may now be contemplating the Crimean War of 1854.

Sir John Penlyon and Mr. Danby had been school-fellows at Eton, and chums at Christchurch; and, whomsoever else he disappointed, Mr. Danby never omitted his annual visits to Penlyon Place. He Christmassed there, and he Eastered there, and he knew the owner of the fine old Tudor house inside and out, his vices and his virtues, his weaknesses, and his prejudices.

"That there Danby," said Sir John's valet, "can turn

the old chap round his finger; but he's a good feller,
is Danby, a gentleman to the marrer, and nobody's any
the worse for 'is hinfluence."

The library at Penlyon was one of those rooms in
which to live seems enough for bliss. A lovely old room,
full of fantastic lights and shadows in the December
gloaming; a spacious room, lined with books in the most
exquisite bindings, for the binding of his books was more
to Sir John than the letterpress inside. He was very
fond of his library; he was very fond of his books. He
looked at the bindings; and he read the newspapers and
magazines which were heaped on a carved oak table at
one end of the room.

Miss Hawberk sat in a low chair, with her feet on the
fender, apparently lost in admiration of her Queen Anne
shoes. She had lately come in from a long walk on the
moor with the useful friend, and had changed her clump-
soled boots for these pointed toes, which set off the high
instep that was considered a family mark of the
Penlyons. A flat-footed Penlyon would have been
thrust out and repudiated by the rest of the clan,

perhaps, like a sick cow to which the herd gives the *coup de grâce*.

Sir John was standing on the hearth-rug with his back to the crackling wood fire, contemplating his books as the fire-glow lit up their varied bindings. Mr. Danby was resting luxuriously after his moorland walk, in quite the most comfortable chair in the room, not too near the fire, for Danby was careful of his complexion. At sixty-three years of age a man, who means to be good-looking to the end, has to be careful of his complexion.

Danby was a slenderly-built man, of middle height. He had never been handsome, but he had neat, inoffensive features, bright grey eyes, light brown hair, with a touch of silver in it, and perfect hands and feet. He reminded elderly people of that accomplished and amiable gentleman, Charles Matthews, the younger.

Miss Hawberk was tall and handsome. She prided herself in the first place upon being every inch a Penlyon, and in the second place upon being undeniably smart. She belonged to a set which, in the London season, sees a good deal of the Royalties, and, like most people who are in touch with personages of the blood royal, she very often talked about them.

So much for the actors in the social drama, which was in this very hour to begin at Penlyon Castle. The curtain is up, and the first words of the play drop quietly from the lips of Sir John.

SIR JOHN. Christmas again, Danby! I think of all the boring seasons Christmas is the most boring.

ADELA (*reproachfully*). My dear uncle, that sounds like forgetting what Christmas means.

SIR JOHN. What does Christmas mean to any British householder? Firstly, an extra Sunday, wedged into the week,—and at my age the longest week is too short, and all the Sundays are too near together; secondly, an overwhelming shower of stationery in the shape of pamphlets, booklets, circulars, and reports of every imaginable kind of philanthropic scheme for extracting money from the well-to-do classes—schemes so many and so various that a man will harden his heart against the cry of the poor rather than he will take the trouble to consider the multitude of institutions that have been invented to relieve their distresses; thirdly, a servants' ball, which generally sets all the servants by the ears, and sometimes sets the house on fire; fourthly, a cloud of letters from poor relatives and friends one would willingly forget, only to be answered decently with a cheque. I won't speak of bills, for the so-called Christmas bills are held back till January, to embitter the beginning of the year, and to remind a man that he was born to trouble, as the sparks fly upward.

Sir John takes up the poker, and illustrates this passage of holy writ by striking a tremendous shower of sparks out of a burning pine log.

DANBY. I don't think *you* need mind Christmas. You are rich enough to satisfy everybody, even the philanthropic gentlemen; or you may plunge for two or three of the best established and soundest charities—hospitals, for choice—and give a round sum to each of them. That is what I would do if I were a rich man. And as for festivities, why, you and I are too old, and Miss Hawberk is too sensible to want any fuss of that kind; so we can just put up with the extra Sunday, and pull up the arrears of our correspondence between luncheon and dinner, while the servants are lingering over their Christmas dessert.

MISS HAWBERK (*with a faint sigh*). That is all very well; but I think Christmas Day ought to be different from other days, somehow.

SIR JOHN (*impatiently*). Somehow, yes, but which how? What are we, civilized people, with plenty of common sense and no silly sentiment—what are we to do year after year in order to lash ourselves into the humour for Christmas mirth and Christmas benevolence? It was all very well for a miserly old churl like Dickens's Scrooge to break out suddenly into kindness and joviality, after a long life of avarice. Giving away turkeys and drinking punch were new sensations for him. But for us, who have been giving away turkeys and putting our sovereigns in the plate for nearly fifty Christmas Days! You can't expect me to be enthusiastic about Christmas, Adela, any more than you would expect me to hang up my stocking when I go to bed on Christmas Eve.

MISS HAWBERK. Oh, that stocking! How old I feel when I think of it! How firmly I believed in Santa Claus, and how happy I used to be on Christmas morning when I found pretty things in my stocking, or heaped up at the end of my bed! The stocking would not hold a quarter of my presents. I know one year when we were at Bournemouth I had a sweet little sketch of a kitten sent by the Hereditary Princess of Kostroma, who was wintering at the Bath for her chest. She had seen me playing in a corner with my kitten a week or two before, when she was taking tea with mother, don't you know.

SIR JOHN (*looking as if he neither knew nor cared about this feline incident*). Stockings, presents, Santa Claus! Ah, there you've hit the mark, Adela. Christmas is a splendid institution in a house where there are children. Christmas can hardly be made too much of where there are children in question. No, Adela, I am not such a heathen as you think. I have not forgotten the meaning of Christmas. I can still remember that it is a festival kept in reverential memory of a Holy Child. If you were not your mother's only daughter and grown up—if somehow or other I had a pack of children belonging to me, I would keep Christmas with the best—keep it as it ought to be kept. But the Penlyons are a vanishing race. I have no children to look to me for gladness.

(*A Silence.*) Adela Hawberk looks at the fire gravely, thoughtfully, mournfully, and a blush mounts to her fair forehead, and slowly fades away. Perhaps she is thinking of a certain young officer in a cavalry regiment, to whom she is not actually engaged, but who may some day be her husband, if the home authorities are agreeable. And she thinks of a dim, far-off time when she and her husband, and possibly their children, may be Christ-massing at Penlyon Castle. The vision seems very remote, almost impossible; yet such things have been. Sir John stares at his books resolutely.

DANBY (*who has been dropping asleep in his dusky corner, rouses himself suddenly*). Children, yes, of course! No-body knows how to enjoy Christmas if he has no children to make happy. If one has no children of one's own, one ought to hire some for the Christmas week—children to cram with mince pies and plum pudding; children to take to the pantomime; children to let off crackers; children to take on the ice. I have any number of god-children scattered about among the houses of my friends, and I feel half a century younger when I am romping with them. What do you think of my notion, Miss Hawberk? Don't you think it would be a good dodge to hire some children for Christmas Day? Your cottages swarm with brats. We should have only to pick and choose.

MISS HAWBERK. Cottagers' children generally have colds in their heads. I don't think one could stand cottagers' children for more than an hour or two. I am very fond of children, but I like them to belong to my own class.

DANBY. I understand. You want little ladies and gentlemen, with whom you could romp at your ease. I believe even that could be managed. What do you say, Sir John? Shall we hire some children for the Christmas week, just to amuse Miss Hawberk?

SIR JOHN. You may do anything in the world that

is idiotic and fantastical, so long as you don't intrude your folly upon me. When you do make a fool of yourself you generally contrive to do the thing pleasantly. If Adela would like some children playing about the house next week, why, she can ask them, or you can ask them; and as long as they behave decently I shall not complain.

DANBY. You don't quite grasp my idea, Sir John. This is not to be a question of inviting children—children out of our own set, spoilt and pampered after the modern fashion, children who would come as guests and would give themselves airs. No. What I propose is to hire some children—children of respectable birth and good manners, but whose parents are poor enough to accept the fee which your liberality may offer for the hire of their olive branches.

SIR JOHN. My dear Danby, the notion is preposterous, —except in St. Giles's, where babies are let out to beggars by the day or week, there can be no such people.

DANBY. There is every kind and grade of people; but one must know where to look for them. Do you

give me permission to hire two or three—say three—
cleanly, respectable children, to assist Miss Hawberk to
get through a solitary Christmas in a lonely country
house, with two old fogies like you and me?

SIR JOHN. That depends. Where do you propose to
find your children? Not in the immediate neighbourhood, unless you want to make me the laughing-stock
of the parish. Amuse yourselves to your hearts' content;
but I must beg you to leave *me* uncompromised by your
foolishness.

MISS HAWBERK. The Sheik is getting .angry, Mr.
Danby. We had better give up your funny idea.

SIR JOHN. No, no, let Danby indulge his fancy.
Danby's fancies are always successful, however absurd
they may seem to reasonable beings.

DANBY (*throwing his head back upon the chair-cushion
and laughing his joyous laugh, a laugh that always puts
other people in good spirits*). There spoke my noble Sheik
—the Prince of Penlyon—the man with the blood of
Cornish kings in his veins. We may have our little bit
of reasonable Christmas festivity, Miss Hawberk and I,

and you won't mind. But how about the fee for the children? We must pay for our little mummers. We must compensate the parents or parent for the sacrifice of Christmas pleasures—the happy morning faces over the stockingful of toys—the glowing evening faces round the humble fireplace, watching the chestnuts roasting on the bars. You don't know what a little world of joy humble folks lose when they don't have their children about them at Christmas.

SIR JOHN. Confound the fee! Give them twenty, fifty pounds, if you like; but don't talk to me of poor children. I will have no poor children at Penlyon. Adela is quite right. They have always colds in their heads; they don't know how to treat decent furniture; they would scroop the heavy chairs on the oak floor; they would leave prints of their horrid little thumbs on my books; and though the imprint of the human thumb may be very interesting to the detective physiologist, I am not a student of thumbs, and I want to keep my books clean.

DANBY. I am not thinking of poor children in your

sense of the word. Though I am thinking of people for whom your cheque, of say fifty pounds, would be a boon.

SIR JOHN. Poor relations of your own, I suppose, Danby. Don't be offended. Everybody has poor relations.

MISS HAWBERK. Dear Princess Romànoff-Moscova has often told me how much she has to do for some of her German connections.

DANBY. You've hit it. I am thinking of some poor relations.

SIR JOHN. Good. If they have any of your blood they are sure to be little ladies and gentlemen. Only— forgive me, Danby—poverty is apt to be pushing. I shall write my cheque for a hundred guineas, since the little people belong to you; but don't let this Christmas visit be the thin end of the wedge. Don't let me hear any more of the little dears, unless I myself wish it.

DANBY. You shall see them and hear of them no more after old Christmas Day, unless at your own desire. Remember it is not a visit. It is a transaction. You hire these little creatures for your amusement—our amusement if you like —just as you would hire a conjuror for a juvenile party. You pay them their fee, and you have done with them.

SIR JOHN. That is as it should be.

Sir John walks across the room to his desk, lights a candle, and writes his cheque, payable to Horatio Danby, for one hundred guineas, while two footmen are bringing in lamps and afternoon tea.

DANBY (*folding up the cheque*). Miss Hawberk, did I not rightly call your uncle a prince?

(*The scene closes.*)

CHAPTER I.

SIR JOHN PEN-
LYON was generally
described by his
friends as a man of
peculiar temper. He
was not a bad-tem-
pered man — indeed,
he had a certain
princely graciousness which overlooked small offences.
He was not easily made angry; but, on the other hand,
when deeply offended, he was vindictive, and nursed his
wrath from year's end to year's end, refusing ever again
to touch the hand of the offender. He had reigned
at Penlyon as a lord of the soil ever since he left the

THE READING OF HIS WIFE'S JOURNAL LEFT IN SIR JOHN PENLYON'S
MIND THE BURDEN OF A LASTING REMORSE.

university, coming into his own at three and twenty
years of age. He had married late, married a very
young woman, dowerless, but of good birth, who loved
him far better than he ever believed during her lifetime.
She died when the younger of her two daughters was
only six years old, and it was some years after she had
been laid at rest in the family vault of the Penlyons
that Sir John found an old diary hidden in a secret
drawer at the back of the secretaire in his wife's dressing-room; a girlish diary, written at intervals; a record
of thoughts and feelings rather than of the facts and
occupations of daily life; a record which told the
widower how fondly he had been beloved, and how
many a careless wound he had inflicted upon that tender
creature whose gentle countenance was hidden from his
sight for ever.

The reading of his wife's journal left in Sir John
Penlyon's mind the burden of a lasting remorse. He
had believed that when the daughter of an impoverished
house, his junior by twenty years, had accepted his
stately offer of marriage, she had been influenced as

much by questions of convenience as he himself had been. He was marrying because the time had come when he ought to marry, unless he wanted to sink into hopeless bachelorhood and loneliness. She was marrying because marriage with a magnate in the land would give her fortune and position. Fixed in this notion of an equality of indifference, he had been studiously polite and kind to his young wife; but he had never taken the trouble to sound the depths of that girlish heart. He had taken everything for granted.

There had been a domestic disappointment, too, in his married life, calm and undisturbed as it was. Two daughters had been born at Penlyon Castle, but no son. And Sir John Penlyon ardently longed for a son. His chief motive in marrying at over forty years of age was the desire of a son and heir. He was angry at the thought that a distant cousin should ever bear his title, and come to reign at Penlyon. The estate was strictly entailed, and that second cousin, a soldier in a line regiment, must needs succeed if Sir John died without leaving a son.

The diary reminded him of many sins; reminded him how cold and unloving he had been to those baby daughters. The mother's girlish handwriting had put every little slight on record; not in anger, but in sorrow. The widower came upon such entries as this: "I think it must be because he does not care for me that he is so neglectful of Lilian. Every one says she is a lovely child. It can't be because I am fond of her that I think her so beautiful. The servants all worship her. Mr. Danby adores her, and she adores him. I couldn't help crying the other day—I had to run out of the room, or I should have made an absolute fool of myself before my husband—when I saw Mr. Danby playing with her, going on his hands and knees under the billiard-table to play at bo-peep with her, just as if he had been her father; while Sir John sat reading his paper at the other end of the room, and only looked up once, to complain of the noise—Lilian's sweet little silvery laugh! How could he call that a noise!"

And this: "I took Sibyl to the library yesterday morning when her father was sitting there alone. It

was her birthday—her third birthday—and I thought I
might presume upon that. I opened the door a little
way and looked in. He was sitting at his desk writing.
I ought to have waited till he was disengaged. I
whispered to her to go to him and give him a big birthday kiss, and she ran in, toddling across the room in her
pretty blue shoes, so busy, so happy, and she caught hold
of his arm as he wrote, and lifted herself up on tiptoe,
and said, 'Papa, big birsday tiss,' in her funny little baby
talk. He put down his pen, and he stooped down to
kiss her; but a moment after he rang his spring bell, two
or three times, and called out, 'What is this child doing
here, roaming about the house alone? Where is her
nurse?' He was very kind and polite when he looked
round and saw me standing at the door, and when I
begged his pardon for having disturbed him; but I could
see that he was bored, and I took Sibyl away directly.
We met Mr. Danby in the corridor with an armful of
toys. What a useful good soul he is, and how sorry I
shall be when he has left us to go to the Duchess at
Endsleigh."

There were many entries of the same nature—womanly regrets, recorded again and again. "I wonder why he married me." "I wonder whether he once loved somebody very dearly and couldn't marry her." "I think there must be some reason for his not caring for me. I ought not to complain, even to this stupid old book—but the book is like an old friend. I sit staring at my name and the date, written by my old governess at the Manor House, and recalling those careless, thoughtless days when my sisters and I used to think our Ollendorff exercises the worst troubles we had in this world—before mother began to be an invalid—before father used to confide all his difficulties to us girls—the debts, the tenants that wouldn't pay, the roofs that wanted new slating. Oh, how long ago it all seems! I have no money troubles now. Father has had legacies, and everything is going smoothly at home. And yet I feel sometimes as if my heart were slowly turning to ice.

> " Break, thou deep vase of chilling tears,
> That time has shaken into frost."

Sir John Penlyon never forgot the reading of that

diary. He remembered the very day and hour when looking for a missing list of family jewels—jewels which his dead wife had worn on state occasions, and which were to go back to the bank, and to lie in darkness, like her who had worn them—he had come upon that old German copy-book, rolled up and thrust far back in the secret drawer, tied with a shabby old ribbon. He remembered sitting by the fireless hearth, in the prettily furnished dressing-room, disused since his wife's death. He remembered the dull grey autumn sky, and the rain drifting across the leaden sea, and the shags standing on the rocks, drenched and drooping, all nature in low spirits.

The reading of that record of unhappiness, so meekly borne, was not without one good result. Sir John took more notice of his two girls than he had ever done in their mother's lifetime. Sibyl, the younger, contrived more particularly to find her way into his heart. She was stronger and more vivacious than her elder sister. She was full of daring, a romp, and a tomboy. Lilian was like her mother, and was gentle, and shrinking, and

SHE WAS FULL OF DARING, A ROMP, AND A TOMBOY.

subdued as her mother had been in the presence of the husband she loved and feared. Sibyl had a nature unacquainted with fear; and her father fancied he saw in her all the highest qualities of the Penlyons—beauty, strength, courage.

"If she had but been a boy," he sometimes said to himself, with a profound sigh.

It seemed a hard thing that such a splendid creature must needs be cheated out of the heritage of her father and grandfather, and of many generations before them. only because she happened to be a daughter instead of a son. The Penlyon estate had been growing in wealth and importance while all those generations of the past were growing from youth to age, through life to death. The Penlyons had developed a great mining district, far off yonder southward towards Truro. They had added farm to farm between Boscastle and Bodmin. Everything had prospered with this proud and ancient race: and from Launceston to Tintagel and Tintagel to Bude there was no such family as the Penlyons of Penlyon Castle.

Sir John was foolishly indulgent to his motherless daughters during the first four or five years of his widowhood, making amends to them for all that had been wanting in his conduct to their mother. His remorse was not for sins of commission, but for sins of omission. He knew that he had not been unkind to his wife. He had only failed to understand her. The poor little diary in the German exercise book had told him how dearly he had been beloved, and how dull and ungrateful he had been.

For nearly five years after his wife's death Sir John lived at Penlyon Castle, managed his estates, hunted and shot, and in summer did a little yachting along that wild north coast, and southward by Penzance and Falmouth, and as far as the Start Point. In all those five years he had his two children much about him, took them on his yacht, taught them to ride, and was enraptured with the pluck and the endurance shown by the younger, whether on sea or land. She rode a pony that her elder sister dared not mount. Her father took her with him when he went out with the harriers, and she rode up and down

those wild hills with a dash and cleverness that enchanted
the squires and farmers of the district.

During all this time the girls were in a manner
running wild. They had a nursery governess to look after
them whose authority was of the smallest, and who soon
came to understand that Sir John Penlyon's daughters
were to do as they liked; and that both learning and
elegant accomplishments counted for very little at
Penlyon Castle.

"Look after their health, Miss Peterson, and see that
they change their shoes when they come in from walking," said Sir John. "All the rest is leather and
prunella."

Miss Peterson, who had never read Pope, took this for
an allusion to the shoes.

The two girls would have got the better of their
governess in any case; but Sir John being avowedly
on the side of ignorance, the poor young lady had no
chance of making them take kindly to education. They
loved the gardens and the hills and the wild sea-beach,
and those narrow walks which looked to Miss Peterson

like mere ledges on the face of the cliff, and where she
could hardly stand for a minute without feeling giddy.
They were strong and bold, and free in every movement
of their young limbs, while she was London-bred, a
weakling, and a very bad walker. Her feet used to ache
on those grand moorland roads, and her poor sick soul
long for a Royal Blue, or any other friendly omnibus,
to take her in and carry her homewards. She was one of
those people who say they are very fond of the country
in summer. The breezy October days, the white
mists of winter, filled her with sadness and dejection.

The two little girls were kind to her after their free-
and-easy fashion; but they treated her with a good-
natured contempt. She was afraid of a horse; she was
afraid of the sea; she was afraid of being blown off the
cliff when the wind was high; and she could not walk
two miles without feeling tired. She confessed to being
troubled with corns.

"Miss Peterson has corns," cried Sibyl; "isn't it
funny? I thought it was only old people who had
corns,"

SHE WAS LONDON-BRED, A VERY BAD WALKER.

D

This free-and-easy life went on for five years. The children throve and grew apace—did what they liked, ate what they liked, and were as idle as they liked. The effect of this indulgence upon their physical health was all that the fondest father could desire. The doctor from Boscastle complained laughingly that the Penlyon nursery wasn't worth a five-pound note to him from year's end to year's end.

"You never have anything the matter with you," he said, as the children skipped round him in the road. fond of him in their small way, as one of the funny personages of the district. "I don't believe I have earned seven and sixpence out of either of you since I lanced your gums."

"Did you lance my gums?" cried Sibyl. "How funny!"

"You didn't think it funny then. I can tell you," said the doctor, grimly.

"Didn't I? What's it like? Lance them now," said Sibyl, curling up her red lips and opening her mouth very wide.

"No, thank you. You'd bite. You look as if you could bite!" laughed the doctor. "I tell you what it is, I believe Miss Peterson is a witch—one of our ancient Cornish witches who has turned herself into a nice-looking young woman." Mr. Nicholls could not so far perjure himself as to say pretty. "Miss Peterson has bewitched you both. She has charmed away the measles and the whooping-cough. She has cheated me out of my just rights."

Miss Peterson heard him with a pale smile, shifting her weight from the more painful foot to the foot that pained her a little less. The children went leaping and bounding along the road, the embodiment of healthy, high-spirited childhood.

Sir John praised Miss Peterson for her care of them, and rewarded her, as the school-board mistresses are rewarded, according to results; only the results in this case were physical and not mental, and Sir John's Christmas present of a silk gown or a ten-pound note was given because his daughters were healthy and happy, rather than because they made any progress with their education. In sober truth, they knew a little less than the village children of the same age at the parish school.

At the end of those five years that pleasant life came to an abrupt close. North Cornwall found out all at once that it could not continue to prosper and to hold its own in the march of progress unless it were represented by Sir John Penlyon. Radical influences were abroad in the land. The Church was in danger, was indeed being fast pushed to the wall by the force of Dissent, its superior in numerical strength. North Cornwall must no longer be given over to the Radical party. It was time that a stand should be made, and a battle should be fought. Sir John Penlyon, said the newspapers, was the man to make that stand, and to fight that battle. He was rich; he had a stake in the country; he was influential; he was fairly popular. He had sat in Parliament fourteen years before for a Cornish borough that was now among the things of the past, a sop long since flung by Conservative Reformers to the Democratic Cerberus. He could never again sit for Blackmount, the hereditary seat of his ancestors, with a constituency of three and twenty; but he could sit for North Cornwall, and North Cornwall claimed him for its own.

Perhaps Sir John Penlyon was getting tired of rusticity. In any case he consented to be nominated in the Conservative interest; and the result of the contest was a triumph for the good old family and the good old cause. Sir John took a small house in Queen Anne's Gate, gave himself up to politics, and almost deserted his Cornish domain. Except for a month or six weeks in the autumn, he was scarcely seen in the West during the seven years that followed his election as Member for the Western Division of North Cornwall. He was re-elected during those seven years without opposition, for it was now felt that the Western Division had become a pocket-borough of the Penlyons, just as Blackmount had been. There was no use in fighting Sir John Penlyon in his stronghold of the west.

Before settling himself in his comfortable bachelor

quarters by St. James's Park, Sir John invited his only sister, Mrs. Hawberk, to Penlyon Place, with a view to taking counsel with her as to the education of his daughters. The time had doubtless come when Lilian and Sibyl must cease to run wild. Mrs. Hawberk's husband was the younger son of a peer, and she gave herself some airs on the strength of that connection. She was very fond of talking of Allerton, the family seat, where she usually spent a somewhat dismal six weeks in September and October while her husband was going about the country speaking at political meetings, and wearing himself out, as he declared, in support of the cause.

Mrs. Hawberk came. She had not seen her nieces since their mother's death. She took them in hand at once in a masterful way; and after spending a single afternoon with them and their governess, she informed her brother that his children were monsters of ignorance.

"The sooner you get rid of that young woman the better," she said of poor Miss Peterson, who had done all in her power to make herself agreeable to the great lady. "She has taught them nothing, and she has not the slightest authority over them."

"She has looked after their health," replied Sir John, apologizing for the governess's shortcomings, "and they are very fond of her."

"One wouldn't wish them to be fond of her. It is a very bad sign when children are fond of their governess. It means that she spoils them and allows them to be idle."

"They have been idle at my desire. I told Miss Peterson to cultivate their bodies and leave their minds alone."

"And she has obeyed you to the letter. I never met with such ignorant children. They pretend to be fond of flowers, yet they know no more of botany than my maid Rogers. They have made no progress with the piano. They know no French. They are backward in everything."

"They are splendid children," said Sir John, doggedly.

"No doubt; and if you allow them to grow up with Miss Peterson they will be splendid savages; and you will be put to shame by them when they go into society. It does not do for girls to be ignorant and unaccomplished nowadays. You will want them to marry well, I suppose, by-and-by ? "

" I shan't want them to marry badly."

" Of course not ; and to make good matches they will have to be accomplished as well as good-looking. They are very sweet girls," added Mrs. Hawberk, not wishing to offend her only brother, and a wealthy brother ; " but they have been dreadfully indulged."

" I wanted them to be happy."

" No doubt they have had a fine time of it. You were not so weak about them in their poor mother's time."

" No ; I wish I had been a little weaker."

" How do you mean ? "

" I think Mary would have liked me to take more notice of them."

" Nonsense, John ; you were perfect in your conduct to poor Mary. No young woman could have had a more chivalrous husband. I hope you don't reproach yourself for having been wanting in any respect towards poor Mary ? "

"Well, we needn't talk about that. Nobody can mend the past. I want you to do what is best for the girls now I am to be so much in London. If Miss Peterson is not governess enough for them she must have a superior person to help her. She can stay to look after their health, and see that they change their shoes."

"My dear John, a maid will do all that. If you want me to be of use to them you must let me have a free hand."

"Certainly; you shall have a free hand for the next five years, till they have finished their education. Lilian is nearly thirteen. Five years hence she will be old enough to enter society."

"And it shall be my care that she is fitted for her position as your eldest daughter," said Mrs. Hawberk, decisively.

CHAPTER II.

SIR JOHN went to London, and left Mrs. Hawberk mistress of the field. She began her work of reform by dismissing meek little Miss Peterson, who was so much afraid of her that she was almost glad to go ; yes, even to exchange the fleshpots of Penlyon Castle for the meagre fare of a lodging in Camden Town. Miss Peterson loved her pupils, and wept at parting from them; but the scornful domination of the fashionable lady had cowed her spirits. She cried bitterly on the last morning at the Castle, but found few words to express either her love or her sorrow.

Sibyl, the impulsive one, clung round Miss Peterson's neck, and abused her aunt for sending this faithful friend away.

"I shall hate the new governess, and I shall always love you," she said.

"My dear, you mustn't hate any one. We have been very happy together, and I hope some day Sir John will let me see you and Lilian again."

"Let you see us!" exclaimed Sibyl; "I should think so, indeed! You shall come and live with me again the minute I am grown up. *She* will have no power over us then."

She was Mrs. Hawberk, who had not left her room at this early hour. The carriage was at the door to take Miss Peterson to the coach, and the coach was to take her to the station at Launceston, whence it would be a long, long journey to Camden Town.

Lilian and Sibyl had packed a picnic basket for her with provisions that would have lasted for a week if the train had been snowed up on the moorland above Okehampton.

"I'll go to Victoria with you," cried Sibyl.

Victoria was the point where the coach stopped to pick up passengers from Penlyon.

"No, no, my darling, your aunt wouldn't like——"

But Sibyl jumped into the carriage before the sentence was finished. The footman shut the door, and the coachman drove off. There was no time to spare, if the coach was to swallow up poor little Miss Peterson that morning.

The coach did swallow her; and Sibyl, without either hat or jacket, alighted from the brougham half an hour afterwards to find her aunt standing in the porch awaiting her return.

"You are the most undisciplined child I ever had to do with," said Mrs. Hawberk.

The new governess arrived three days after Miss Peterson's departure. She, too, was young in years; but she was old in culture and accomplishments. She was a model governess. She had taken prizes and certificates, and had passed examinations of all kinds. She was strong in mathematics and in natural science. She knew a respectable amount of Latin, and had a useful smattering of Greek—enough to make her oppressively erudite about the derivation of words. Sibyl and Lilian began by hating her, and though hatred soon simmered down to toleration, they never became fond of her. She had indifferent health, and suffered from neuralgic headaches; and indeed it seemed as if she introduced headaches into Penlyon Place, for her pupils very soon began to suffer from aching temples, and to look dark and heavy about the eyes, and to lose those fine appetites for indiscriminate food which they had enjoyed under the Peterson *régime*, in the old happy time when they used to go down to dessert every evening and sit on each side of their father, and eat as much fruit and cake, chow-chow, guava jelly, and preserved pine-apple as ever they liked, while Sir John nibbled an olive or two, and sipped his claret.

Neuralgia and headache reigned at Penlyon; and the two girls grew white and wan, like their all-accomplished governess; and Mr. Nicholls, the family doctor, had no

longer to complain of the rude health of the Miss
Penlyons. He had plenty of visits booked against
Penlyon Place at the end of the year.

Just at the time when Lilian and Sibyl were growing
fastest, running up from stout, chubby children, into thin
slips of girls; just when their constitutions most needed
rest, and liberty, and pleasant exercise in the open air—
riding, tennis, walking, rowing, romping—this burden of
education was laid upon them. They were reminded
every day that they had been neglected, and that they
were to make amends for lost time by extra application.
They were crammed with 'ologies from which not one
young woman out of a hundred ever derives the faintest
pleasure or advantage in after-life. They were made to
sit at the piano, tap, tap, tapping the notes, first with one
finger and then with another, in monotonous five-finger
exercises—the athletics of piano practice, Miss Gambert
called this heart-sickening drudgery. Even the music
they played as a relief from the five-finger tapping was of
a dry and learned order which aroused no interest in their
minds—a "sad, mechanic exercise," and no more. Their

only pleasure at the piano was found in stolen minutes, when Miss Gambert was out of ear-shot, when Sibyl, whose ear was of the quickest, picked out music-hall tunes, which she had heard gardeners or stable-boys whistling at their work. Music-hall ditties that catch the fancy of city and suburbs will travel even as far west as Tintagel.

Mr. Nicholls remonstrated with the governess upon the subject of over-much study, and had even the audacity to argue the point with Mrs. Hawberk herself, on one of her half-yearly visits to Penlyon Place.

That lady laughed his arguments to scorn.

" We have got beyond that old-fashioned idea of brain-work being bad for the constitution, my good Mr. Nicholls. Look at judges, bishops, famous physicians, some of the longest-lived men on record. My nieces are like all girls of their age, fanciful and rather affected. Miss Gambert is giving them a sound and solid education, which will make them valuable members of society ; and here you come with your old-fashioned fads about over-work and mental strain."

" I can only tell, you, madam, that these dear young

ladies have deteriorated in health since Miss Peterson
left—— "

" Miss Peterson! She was a favourite of yours,
evidently, doctor," interrupted Mrs. Hawberk, with a
sneer which brought an indignant blush to the cheeks
and forehead of the bachelor doctor, who had never given
Miss Peterson so much as a thought in the way of
gallantry. " Come, Mr. Nicholls, in spite of your worship
of ignorance, I think you will admit that any deterioration
in my nieces is the effect of over-growth, and that it is
natural for girls of their age to be weak and weedy."

" Yes, Mrs. Hawberk, and that weak and weedy age is
just the period at which the educational strain should be
relaxed. However, I can but submit to your superior
wisdom, and hope that with the help of tonics and a
strengthening diet the young ladies may regain the
ground lost in the last year or so."

" Give them as many tonics as you like; only don't
interfere with the cultivation of their minds."

Mrs. Hawberk took her own way in this as in every
other matter in which she was given what she called a

E

free hand. She had an invincible belief in her own wisdom, and in the foolishness of almost everybody else. She drove Miss Gambert, and Miss Gambert drove her pupils, and Lilian Penlyon at eighteen years of age was certainly a very well read and accomplished young woman, only it was a pity that she should be so weak and weedy, and consumptive-looking.

"Her poor mother's constitution," Mrs. Hawberk said decisively, when Sir John lamented his daughter's delicate health.

Lilian made her *début* in society, chaperoned by her aunt, from a fine house in the best part of Cromwell Road, while Sibyl stayed at Penlyon, and went on grinding at the dry-as-dust books, and the learned German music, which the most advanced educational authorities had prescribed for the cultivation of youthful minds. Lilian went everywhere, and was admired for her delicate beauty and the shy dignity of her manners, and her unlikeness to other girls. She had grown up in solitude, and the slang of other girls was a language unknown to her, and the ways of other girls were foreign to her mind. She was very much admired for these superior qualities, and it was not forgotten that she was joint heiress of Sir John Penlyon, the wealthy Cornishman, whose mines and slate quarries were known to yield a large revenue, without counting his extensive landed estate, the greater part of which unhappily was included in the entail, and would go to the heir-at-law. Before Lilian had been out three months Mrs. Hawberk had the triumph of informing her brother that Lord Lurgrave, the Earl of Holmsley's son, had proposed to his elder daughter, and only waited his permission to consider himself formally engaged to her.

"Does Lilian like the young man?" Sir John asked briefly.

"I believe it is quite a romantic attachment on both sides."

"Then let them marry," said Sir John; "the sooner the better."

He did everything in his power to facilitate the marriage. The young man was a good young man. Nobody had any charge to bring against him; and his father, Lord Holmsley, was well placed in the world, and stood well with the world. The alliance was altogether honourable ; and Miss Penlyon was thought to have done well for herself in her first season.

Sir John had his own reasons for hurrying on the marriage, reasons which he told to nobody. More than once during the years of his widowhood he had been on the point of taking a second wife, and at the eleventh hour, on the eve of proposing to a lady whom he thought inclined to favour his suit, he had drawn back. No, he had married once without love, and he had not made his wife happy. He would not enter upon a second loveless union in the hope of an heir to his estate. Long ago, in his early manhood, he had loved, and he had been balked in his love, which had been bestowed upon one who was his inferior in birth and social status. He had loved a farmer's daughter, and had wanted to make her his wife, setting all social distinctions at nought for her dear sake. But he had given her up at his father's bidding, and at her own entreaty. She loved him too well to make bad blood between father and son.

All this had happened nearly forty years ago, but it had influenced the whole of Sir John Penlyon's after life. He made up his mind that there should be no second loveless union for him, and he looked forward to seeing his grandchildren grow up about him. He could not give Penlyon Place or the lands of Penlyon to his daughter's son. Those must go to the heir-at-law; but he might bequeath the accumulations of long years, and the quarries and mines which he himself had bought. He had never spent more than a third of his income.

When he went down to the west in October he found Mrs. Hawberk established there before him, superintending all the domestic arrangements for the marriage. The wedding clothes were being made in London. All that Sir John had to do was to agree with Lord Holmsley's lawyers about the settlement. The wedding was fixed for the fifteenth of November. The settlement was liberal, but if Sir John Penlyon's daughter were to die childless, her fortune would revert to her father, and young Lord Lurgrave would have nothing. This point was insisted upon by Sir John's lawyer.

"Happily the young lady's death is a remote contingency," said Lord Holmsley, when his own lawyer objected to the clause.

Sir John found the lovers very happy, and Penlyon Place in a pleasant bustle of expectation. He found Sibyl still grinding on at science and history, and more 'ologies than he himself had ever heard of, a university education in his day not having recognized the 'ologies. He found her pale and thin, and disguised in smoke-coloured spectacles, which she had taken to wearing because the light hurt her eyes.

"My poor pretty Sibyl, how they have changed you!" exclaimed Sir John.

His younger daughter, once so daring in her merriment, so frankly demonstrative in her affection, was now shy and restrained in her manner to her father. He had seen a good deal of Lilian in the London season; and the ice had been broken between them. Lilian was almost the Lilian of old. But Sibyl was completely changed; and though Mrs. Hawberk assured him that the change was an improvement, he could not help regretting the old Sibyl, the frank and fearless companion, the spirited young horsewoman, the sunburnt, bronze-haired girl who could handle oar or boat-hook with the best of the lads of Boscastle. He saw her at her studies in the library every morning; he heard her play erudite German music after dinner in the drawing-room. He saw her and Miss Gambert setting out every afternoon for their constitutional walk on the moors, and riding home in the dusk one evening he saw them pacing the windblown road with Mr. Morland, the High Church curate, in attendance. He questioned Sibyl about the curate when she had played her newest mazurka and was bidding him good-night.

"Is there anything between Miss Gambert and Morland?" he asked. "Is he paying his addresses to her?"

"No, father, I think not."

"Humph; I began to suspect something when I saw him walking with you two this afternoon. He is a very good fellow, though his father is only a grocer in a small way of business in Plymouth. She might do worse."

"Yes, he is very good."

That was all. Sibyl touched her father's cheek with a faint fluttering kiss and retired, leaving the room in the quiet manner which Miss Gambert had impressed upon her as the proper manner for a young lady belonging to one of the county families.

Miss Penlyon's wedding was a very smart wedding, or as smart as a wedding can be in the wilds of Cornwall. She had a bishop to marry her, assisted by a High Church archdeacon, and by Mr. Morland, curate of the parish—Mr. Morland, who was a pale, thin young man with large blue eyes and a short, nervous cough, and who was nearer Rome in all his thoughts and aspirations than the archdeacon.

Lilian Penlyon was as graceful and dignified a bride as any one could desire to see; and Mrs. Hawberk prided herself upon the result of her wise administration.

"I hope you are satisfied with your daughters to-day, John," she said, swelling with conscious merit, her matronly form seeming larger than usual in the amplitude of a brand new velvet gown.

"They are looking very handsome; but I wish they did not look so fragile," replied Sir John, gravely.

"Blood, my dear John, blood. You wouldn't expect a racer to show the bulk and bone of a carthorse."

When the wedding was over, and Lilian and her husband were travelling in Italy on a wedding tour which was to last till the spring, life at Penlyon Castle dropped back into the old grooves; and the old grooves meant books and piano and drawing-board, varied only by the dull constitutional walk or the duller drive. The winter skies in that western land were clear and bright, and a few stray flowers lingered here and there in the shelter of the hills, as if winter had forgotten them; but the landscape in all its poetic beauty was a melancholy landscape for the afternoon eyes of a girl, whose long laborious mornings were given to dry books and drier music, and to convincing herself with strenuous toil that she had no talent for painting.

The daily walk was insisted upon by doctor and governess; so Miss Penlyon was marched out in fair weather or foul, and had to tramp submissively for at least four miles, sometimes buffeted by the wind and the spray, sometimes moving ghost-like in a grey mist of rain.

Mr. Morland, the curate, often joined governess and pupil in these afternoon walks. He had nothing to say about the world of men, but he had lived and had his being from boyhood upwards in a little world of books, and about these he was eloquent. Carlyle, Emerson, Hawthorne, Longfellow, Shelley, Keats—these were his gods, and he would quote them and talk of them for an hour at a stretch.

To Sibyl, who had been reared upon hard facts strictly on the Gradgrind principle, the world of philosophy and poetry was a revelation. She explored her father's library, and in a corner among the very refuse of the shelves found a shabby old volume of Shelley, printed in Paris ; and this treasure she carried off to her bedroom and kept under her pillow and pored over in secret, marking *his* favourite passages and learning them by rote ; so that one day, half unconsciously, she took up the line where Mr. Morland stopped, and went on to the end of the stanza.

"I hope you found those lines in a book of selections," said Miss Gambert. "I am sure your aunt would disapprove of Shelley."

"She may disapprove, but I'm sure she never read him," answered Sibyl. "Lilian told me that she never reads anything but the tradesmen's books, and that she pores over them every Tuesday morning in a maddening manner, and then has awful talks with her housekeeper."

"Mrs. Hawberk is a very clever woman and an admirable manager."

"I dare say she is; but she need not parade her butcher's book. She has a pile of horrid tradesmen's books on the breakfast table, and looks over them as she eats her breakfast. I call it absolutely indecent. Lilian said it made her hate Tuesday mornings. She used to wonder if aunt thought she made too much difference in the weekly bills."

"Mrs. Hawberk has ample means, and keeps a liberal table; but she abhors waste, as all sensible women do," said the governess, reprovingly.

"If she parades her butcher's book when I am in the

Cromwell Road I shall say something rude to her,"
retorted Sibyl; "but I hope Lilian will be in town in
the spring, and then she will be able to chaperon
me."

"You are looking forward eagerly to the spring,
when you will have left Cornwall," said Mr. Morland,
pensively; and then there came a silence upon Sibyl
and the curate, and Miss Gambert did all the talking
during the homeward walk.

Sir John Penlyon went back to London soon after
Christmas, and politics claimed him for their own. He
had arranged with his sister that Sibyl was to make her
début from the Cromwell Road as Lilian had done. Lady
Lurgrave, even if she were to have a house in town,
which was doubtful, would be too young and inexperienced
a matron to take charge of her sister. She would not
have the firmness of will needed to keep younger sons
at bay; she would be too good-natured and easy in her
treatment of detrimentals: altogether Sir John felt that
his sister would be the only competent chaperon for
Sibyl, whom he always thought of as wild and difficult to

manage, remembering how rash and wilful she had been
in those childish years, when she rode the piebald pony,
and insisted upon going faster at ditches and hedges than
her father thought safe for so juvenile a performer. She
had been headstrong and disobedient in those days; but
he had loved her for her high spirits and daring. Now
on the threshold of womanhood she was obedient enough
to please the most exacting parent. Mrs. Hawberk and
Miss Gambert between them had succeeded in taming
her; but perhaps Sir John hardly liked this younger
daughter of his quite so well after that careful training
as he had liked her in her childhood, when she had been
as wild and sweet as a dog-rose and as full of thorns.
Mrs. Hawberk, however, took credit to herself for having
produced the most perfect thing in young ladies; and
Sir John felt that he ought to be grateful.

He really did feel grateful to this clever sister of his
for having taken all his paternal responsibilities off his
shoulders and left him free to attend to the affairs of the
nation—very grateful, until one foggy afternoon in
February when a telegram was brought to him in

the library at the Carlton, where he was writing his letters.

"To Sir John Penlyon.

"Sibyl left the castle at seven this morning. She has been traced as far as Bodmin-road Station; supposed to have gone to Bristol. I am in the greatest distress of mind. Pray tell me what I am to do.

"GAMBERT."

"What does the woman mean?" Sir John asked himself, staring at the words in the telegram. "Sibyl must have quarrelled with her, and is on her way to London, meaning no doubt to come to her aunt or to me. Bristol is all nonsense—a mistake of the porters or of the servant who followed her to Bodmin. A foolish, trouble-some business—just now, too, with this amendment coming on to-night, and when I am so full of work."

He looked at his watch. Half-past two. The train from Bodmin would arrive at Paddington soon after four. He must be on the platform, of course, to receive this foolish daughter. It was very wrong of her—a vein of the old Adam cropping up in the regenerate Sibyl. Who would have thought her capable of such rebellion?

"She seemed so tame and well broken when I was at Penlyon," mused Sir John, "but no doubt that middle-aged young lady with the spectacles and the scraggy shoulders is rather a trying person to live with, in a country house, through a long winter."

He went on writing his letters till there was only just time to get to Paddington, allowing a widish margin for the fog—before the fast train from the far west came in. If the train also had not been delayed by the fog, Sir John would not have been there to see its arrival.

He was there, walking up and down the platform, watchful and on the alert, until the last cab had driven away with the last passenger and the last portmanteau; but among all those passengers there was no daughter of his.

"I am a fool," he said to himself; "she may have got out at Westbourne Park."

He took another cab and had himself driven slowly through the thickening fog across the park to South

Kensington and the fine large house in the Cromwell Road, from which Sibyl was to take a header into London society.

Mrs. Hawberk was sitting alone in the subdued lamplight of the back drawing-room, the spacious front drawing-room a yawning gulf of shadows lighted only by occasional gleams from a low fire.

She started from her chair as Sir John was announced, and ran to him and fell upon his neck sobbing—

"Oh, my dear, dear John, I am so sorry for you," she exclaimed gaspingly.

"What do you mean, Clara? What has happened? Has Sibyl come to you?"

"Come to me, poor blind, deluded girl! Come to me? Oh, John, haven't you heard? Didn't you receive poor Miss Gambert's second telegram?"

"No!" cried Sir John, fiercely. "What does it all mean? Has there been an accident on the line? Is the girl hurt—killed?" he asked, hoarse with sudden terror.

His sister's tears, her agitation, her embraces were enough to suggest direst calamity.

"Killed!" cried Mrs. Hawberk. "No, she is safe
enough. There are some parents, perhaps, who would
rather hear that she had been killed in a railway accident

" CLARA, IF YOU WOULD BE GOOD ENOUGH TO TELL ME IN PLAIN WORDS
WHAT HAS HAPPENED, INSTEAD OF TRYING TO ACT LIKE MADAME
RISTORI IN ' MEDEA,' YOU WOULD DO ME A FAVOUR."

than that she had so lowered herself, thrown herself
away so blindly as she has done!"

"Clara, if you would be good enough to tell me in plain
words what has happened to my daughter, instead of
trying to act like Madame Ristori in *Medea*, you would do
me a favour," said Sir John, in his most unpleasant voice.

F

Mrs. Hawberk sat down and collected herself, thinking, as she did so, that it was in the fraternal nature to be disagreeable at every stage of life. She remembered dimly how shamefully her brother had ill-treated her favourite doll five and forty years before. He was the same man now—now, after she had toiled and slaved for him, saving him all thought and care about his motherless girls. The same man, utterly heartless and unfeeling.

"Your daughter Sibyl was married to Mr. Morland, the curate, at St. Sophia's Church, Plymouth, this morning," she said with haughty indifference. "If you haven't received your own telegram, you may like to see mine."

She waved her hand towards an occasional table, on which lay an open telegram. Sir John snatched it up and read it eagerly, stooping to get the light of the shaded lamp, which was intended to make darkness visible rather than to illuminate the room.

"The inquiries about Bristol were only a blind. She went to Plymouth with Mr. Morland, and they were married at St. Sophia's, and have gone to Torquay for their honeymoon. A telegram from him to me—letter

STOLEN HOURS IN THE GARDEN AT PLACE.

to follow. Also letter to Sir John. I think you must feel for me, dear friend, for you alone can understand my feelings under this cruel blow."

It was a long telegram. A woman must be deeply moved before she can be so reckless in the expenditure of words, every one of which has to be paid for.

"Her feelings!" growled Sir John; "what have her feelings to do with my daughter's misconduct, except so far as she has proved herself unworthy of being trusted with the care of a pupil?"

"Oh, John! don't you know the poor thing was engaged to Morland? He pretended to be only waiting for his first living in order to marry her."

"Oh, that was the state of the case, was it?" said Sir John, with cutting coolness. "And he thought it a better speculation to marry my daughter. I am very sorry for him. He will find he has made a bad bargain. He would have done better to marry the governess, for she is a bread-winner, and my daughter will never bring him a sixpence."

"Oh, John! She has been very foolish, poor child, but I know you will forgive her—after a time."

"Not after an eternity—if eternity could have an afterwards. She has set me at nought, and from this hour to my last hour on earth I shall set her at nought. It shall be to me as if she had never existed."

CHAPTER III.

THE time, after-
noon — the after-
noon of Christmas
Eve; the place, the
library at Penlyon
Castle ; and the
only personage Sir John Penlyon, sitting by the fire
in the gathering dusk, somewhat out of temper with
the world at large, and with himself as the most important member in it. The morning had been trouble-
some, spent for the most part with his bailiff, who was
full of the wants and the shortcomings of tenants. Sir
John had missed his useful friend Danby, and that
philosophical spirit which always made light of such

thorns in the flower-bed of a rich man's lot, and always succeeded in laughing him out of his bad temper.

Mr. Danby had been absent for the last four days.

He had gone, with Sir John's cheque in his pocket, to fetch the Christmas hirelings; the little people who were to come to the dull old castle and make merriment for its solitary lord.

The more Sir John Penlyon meditated upon the business, especially this afternoon, the more preposterous and vexatious it seemed to him.

"I must have been an arrant fool to consent to such a piece of folly," he said to himself.

Enter ADELA HAWBERK, *flushed and excited.*

ADELA. We have finished, uncle (*clapping her hands*). It is quite the prettiest tree you ever saw. How delighted the dear little things will be!

SIR JOHN (*testily*). Dear little things, indeed! How do you know they mayn't be odious little things, spoilt and cantankerous, or underbred and hypocritical, if they have been what a middle-class mother calls " well brought up "—brought up to sit upon the edge of their chair, and to be afraid of everybody ?

Adela (*with conviction*). They are sure to be nice children. Mr. Danby wouldn't bring nasty ones.

Sir John. What does he know about children—an old bachelor ?

Adela. Why, uncle, you can't have seen him in a children's party, or you'd never say that. He is a prodigious favourite with the children in all the houses he goes to. Perhaps that is one reason why the mothers are so fond of him. Hark ! They ought to be here by this time. The carriage went to Victoria an hour ago to meet the coach from Launceston. They were to stay at Plymouth last night. Mr. Danby thought it would be too long a journey for the little things to do in one day. He is so considerate.

Sir John. He is a fool; and I am a greater fool to encourage his nonsense. The utter absurdity of bringing children from the other end of the world ! Do you know where the creatures come from, Adela ?

ADELA. I haven't the faintest notion. All Mr. Danby said was that they lived on the other side of London, and that he wanted a clear week to fetch them. You must remember, uncle, you told him you wanted to know nothing about them. They were to come and go, and you were to hear no more of them. They were to have no claim upon you in the future.

SIR JOHN. I should think not, indeed. Claim upon me, forsooth! But it would have been only civil to tell me where the brats come from, and who their people are.

ADELA. No doubt he will tell you, if you ask him.

SIR JOHN. He ought to have told me of his own accord. I am not going to ask him.

Adela was discreetly silent, seeing that her uncle was in what she called one of his tempers. She always respected her uncle's tempers.

She went to the big bay window from which she could see a long way down the drive. It was not four o'clock, but the dimness of a wintry twilight was creeping over the landscape. The afternoon was mild and calm, by no means an old-fashioned Christmas, an afternoon that might have been October. She could hear a faint sighing of the wind in the trees near at hand, and the roaring

of the waves far off, not a stormy roar, only the rhythmical rise and swell of the great Atlantic rolling over the stony beach.

Everything had been made ready for the little strangers. There were fires blazing in two large bedrooms overhead; rooms with a door of communication. In one there were still

IN EAST LONDON.

the two little white beds in which Lilian and Sibyl had slept when they were children; poor Lilian, whose bed was in the English cemetery at Florence, under a white marble monument erected by her sorrowing husband, and whose sorrowing husband had taken to himself a second wife five years ago. Every one knew where Lilian was lying; but no one at Penlyon Castle knew where Sibyl's head had found rest. All that people knew about the disobedient daughter was that her husband had died within three or four years of her marriage, worn to death in some foreign mission, after toiling for a year or so at the east end of London. Of his luckless widow no one at Penlyon had heard anything, but it was surmised that her father made her an allowance. He could hardly let his only daughter starve, people said, however badly she might have treated him. Lady Lurgrave's early death had been a crushing blow to his love and to his pride. She had died childless.

The rooms were ready. Adela ran upstairs to take a final survey. One of the housemaids had been told off to wait upon the little strangers; and Adela's maid was to give a hand. Neither of these young women had any objection to the extra duty. Each professed herself fond of children.

"They'll enliven the place a little, poor mites," said Harrop, who considered Penlyon the abode of dullness; and Sarah the housemaid agreed with her.

Harrop was to sleep in the larger room, and in the bed which Miss Peterson had occupied during five peaceful years. Sarah had put up her truckle bed in the inner and smaller room, where she was to keep guard over the little boy.

"It would be downright cruelty to let any child sleep alone in one of these gashly rooms," said Sarah, the "gashliness" being doubtless a question of spaciousness and oak panelling, and ponderous old-fashioned furniture which cast monstrous shadows in the pale glimmer of the night-light.

Hark! Yes, that was the roll of wheels on the gravel drive, a nearer sound than the sullen swell of the sea out yonder grinding the pebbles in an unresting mill.

Adela Hawberk flew down to the hall, followed by Harrop, while Sarah the housemaid stopped upstairs and gave a final stir to the fires after the wont of her tribe, who are always ready to use the poker, wanted or not wanted, with a noble disregard to the coal-merchant's bill.

Sir John had heard the carriage stop, and the opening of the hall door; and although he pretended to go on reading his paper by the lamp placed close at his elbow, the pretence was a poor one, and anybody might have seen that he was listening with all his might.

The footman had opened the hall door as the wheels drew near, and it was wide open when the carriage stopped. The red light from the hall fire streamed out upon the evening grey, and three little silvery voices were heard exclaiming—

"Oh, what a pretty house!"

"Oh, what a big house!"

And then the smallest voice of the three, with amazing distinctness—

"What an exceedingly red fire!"

The carriage door flew open, and two little girls, all in red from top to toe, and one little boy in grey, rolled out in a heap, or seemed to roll out, like puppies out of a basket, and scrambled on to their feet, and ran up the steps, Mr. Danby, slim and jaunty as usual, following them.

"Good gracious, how tiny they are!" cried Adela, stooping down to kiss the smaller girl, a round red bundle, with a round little face. and large dark grey eyes shining in the firelight.

The tiny thing accepted the kiss somewhat shrinkingly. and looked about her, awed by the grandeur of the hall, the large fireplace and blazing logs, the men in armour, or the suits of armour standing up and pretending to be men.

"I don't like them," said the tiny girl, clinging to Danby, and pointing with a muffled red hand at one of these mailed warriors. "They're not alive, are they, Uncle Tom?"

"No, no, no, Moppet; they're as dead as door-nails."

"Are they? I don't like dead people."

"Come, come, Moppet, suppose they're not people at all—no more than a rocking-horse is a real live

horse. We'll pull one of them down to-morrow and look inside him; and then you'll be satisfied."

The larger scarlet mite, larger by about an inch, older by a year, was standing before the fire, gravely warming her hands, spreading them out before the blaze as much as hands so tiny could spread themselves. The boy was skipping about the hall, looking at everything, the armed warriors especially, and not at all afraid.

"They're soldiers, aren't they?" he asked.

"Yes, Laddie."

"I should like to be dressed like that, and go into a battle and kill lots of people. I couldn't be killed myself, could I, if I had that stuff all over me?"

"Perhaps not, Laddie; but I don't think it would answer. You'd be an anachronism."

"I wouldn't mind being a nackerism if it saved me from being killed," said Laddie.

"Come, little ones, come and be presented to your host," said Mr. Danby, as the footman opened the library door; and they all poured in, Danby, Adela, and the children, the smallest running in first, her sister and the boy following, considerably in advance of the grown-ups.

Moppet ran right into the middle of the room, as fast as her little red legs could carry her, then seeing Sir John sitting where the bright lamplight shone full upon his pale elderly face, with its strongly marked features, black eyebrows, and silvery grey hair, she stopped suddenly as if she had beheld a Gorgon, and began to back slowly till she brought herself up against the silken skirt of Adela Hawberk's gown, and in that soft drapery she in a manner absorbed herself, till there was nothing to be seen of the little neatly rounded figure except the tip of a bright red cap, and the toes of two bright red gaiters.

The elder mite had advanced less boldly, and had not to beat so ignominious a retreat. She was near enough to Mr. Danby to clutch his hand, and holding that, she was hardly at all frightened.

The boy, older, bolder, and less sensitive than either of the girls, went skipping round the library as he had skipped about the hall, looking at things and apparently unconscious of Sir John Penlyon's existence.

" How d'ye do, Danby ? " said Sir John, holding out his hand as his old friend advanced to the fire, the little red girl hanging on to his left hand, while he gave his right to his host. " Upon my word, I began to think you were never coming back. You've been an unconscionable time. One would suppose you had to fetch the children from the world's end."

"I had to bring them to the world's end, you might say. Boscastle is something more than a day's journey from London in the depth of winter."

"And are these the children? Good heavens, Danby! What could you be thinking about to bring us such morsels of humanity?"

"We wanted children," said Danby, "not hobbledehoys."

"Hobbledehoys! no, but there is reason in everything. You couldn't suppose I wanted infants like these—look at that little scrap hidden in Adela's frock. It's positively dreadful to contemplate! They will be getting under my feet. I shall be treading upon them, and hurting them seriously."

"No you won't, Jack, I'll answer for that."

"Why not, pray?"

"Because of their individuality. They are small, but they are people. When Moppet comes into a room everybody knows she is there. She is a little scared now; but she will be as bold as brass in a quarter of an hour."

Sir John Penlyon put on his spectacles and looked at

G

the little hirelings more critically. Their youth and diminutive size had been a shock to him. He had expected bouncing children, with rosy faces, long auburn hair, and a good deal of well-developed leg showing below a short frock. These, measured against his expectations, were positively microscopic.

Their cheeks were pale rather than rosy. Their hair was neither auburn nor long. It was dark hair, and it was cropped close to the neat little heads, showing every bump in the broad, clever-looking foreheads. Sir John's disapproving eyes showed him that the children were more intelligent than the common run of children; but for the moment he was not disposed to accept intelligence instead of size.

"They are preposterously small," he said, "not at all the kind of thing I expected. They will get lost under chairs or buried alive in waste-paper baskets. I wash my hands of them. Take them away, Adela. Let them be fed and put to bed;" then turning to Mr. Danby as if to dismiss the subject, "Anything stirring in London when you were there, Tom?"

Before Danby could answer, Moppet emerged from her shelter, advanced deliberately, and planted herself in front of Sir John Penlyon, looking him straight in the face.

"I'm sorry you don't like us, Mr. Old Gentleman," she said.

Every syllable came with clear precision from those infantine lips. Moppet's strong point was her power of speech. Firm, decisive, correct as to intonation, came every sentence from the lips of this small personage. Ponderous polysyllables were no trouble to Moppet. There was only an occasional consonant that baffled her.

"Who says I don't like you?" said Sir John, taken aback, and lifting the animated bundle of red cloth on to his knee.

He found there was something very substantial inside the woolly cloak and gaiters, a pair of round plump arms and sturdy little legs, a compact little figure, which perched firmly on his knee.

"You said so," retorted Moppet, with her large grey

eyes very wide open, and looking full into his. "You don't like us because we are so very small. Everybody says we are small, but everybody doesn't mind. Why do you mind?"

"I didn't say anything about not liking you, little one. I was only afraid you were too small to go out visiting."

"I went out to tea when I was two, and nobody said I was too small. I have real tea at parties, not milk-and-water. And I have been out to tea often and often—haven't I, Lassie?"

"Not so many times as I have," replied the elder red thing, with dignity.

She was standing in front of the wide old fireplace, warming her hands, and she was to Sir John's eye somewhat suggestive of a robin redbreast that had fluttered in and lighted there.

"Of course not, because you're older," said Moppet, disgusted at this superfluous self-assertion on her sister's part. "I am always good at parties—ain't I, Uncle Tom?" turning an appealing face to Mr. Danby.

"So these Lilliputians are your nieces, Danby?" exclaimed Sir John.

"Well, no, they are not exactly nieces, though they are very near and dear. I am only a jury uncle."

"A jury uncle!" cried Moppet, throwing her head back and laughing at the unknown word.

"A jury uncle!" echoed the other two, and the three laughed prodigiously, not because they attached any meaning to the word, but only because they didn't know what it meant. That was where the joke lay.

"You know that in Cornwall and in Sicily all the elderly men are uncles, and all the old women aunts; everybody's uncles and aunts," concluded Mr. Danby.

Moppet still occupied Sir John's knee. She felt somehow that it was a post of honour, and she had no inclination to surrender it. Her tiny fingers had possessed themselves of his watch-chain.

"Please show me your watch." she said.

Sir John drew out a big hunter.

Moppet approached her little rosy mouth to the hinge and blew violently.

"Why don't it open like Uncle Tom's watch does when I blow?" she asked. "Is it broken?"

"Blow again, and we'll see about that," said Sir John, understanding the manœuvre.

The big bright case flew open as Moppet blew.

"Take care it doesn't bite your nose off."

"How big and bright it is—much bigger and brighter than Uncle Tom's."

"Uncle Tom's is a lady's watch, and Uncle Tom is a lady's man," said Sir John, and the triple peal of childish laughter which greeted this remark made him fancy himself a wit.

Small as they were these children were easily amused, and that was a point in their favour, he thought.

"Tea is ready in the breakfast-room," said Adela.

"Tea in the breakfast-room! Oh, how funny!" And again they all laughed.

At any rate they were not doleful children—no long faces, no homesick airs, no bilious headaches—so far.

"I dare say they will all start measles or whooping-cough before we have done with them," thought Sir John, determined not to be hopeful.

"Oh, we are to come to tea, are we?" he said cheerily, and he actually carried Moppet all the way to the breakfast-room, almost at the other end of the rambling old house, and planted her in a chair by his side at the tea-table. She nestled up close beside him.

"You like us now, don't you?" she asked.

"I like you."

"And you'll like her," pointing to her sister with a small distinct finger; "and him," pointing to her brother, "to-morrow morning. You'll know us all to-morrow morning."

"To-morrow will be Christmas," said Laddie, as if giving a piece of useful information to the company in general.

"Christmas!" cried Danby; "so it will. I mustn't forget to hang up my stocking."

This provoked a burst of mirth. Uncle Tom's stocking! Uncle Tom hoping to get anything from Santa Claus!

"You needn't laugh," said Mr. Danby, seriously. "I mean to hang up one of my big Inverness stockings. It will hold a lot."

"What do you expect to get?" asked Laddie, intensely amused. "Toys?"

"No; chocolates, butterscotch, hardbake, alecompane."

"Oh, what's alecompane?"

The name of this old-fashioned sweetmeat was received with derision.

"Why, what an old sweet-tooth you must be!" exclaimed Moppet; "but I don't believe you a bit. I shall come in the middle of the night to see if your stocking is there."

"You won't find my room. You'll go into the wrong room most likely, and find one of the three bears."

Moppet laughed at the notion of those familiar beasts. "There never were three bears that lived in a house, and had beds and chairs and knives and forks and things," she said. "I used to believe it once when I was very little" —she said *veway* little; "but now I know it isn't true."

She looked round the table with a solemn air, with her

SIR JOHN WATCHED HER CURIOUSLY.

lips pursed up, challenging contradiction. Her quaint
little face, in which the forehead somewhat overbalanced
the tiny features below it, was all aglow with mind. One
could not imagine more mind in any living creature than
was compressed within this quaint scrap of humanity.

Sir John watched her curiously. He had no experience
of children of that early age. His own daughters had
been some years older before he began to notice them. He
could but wonder at this quick and eager brain animating
so infinitesimal a body.

Moppet looked round the table; and what a table it
was! She had never seen anything like it. Cornwall,
like Scotland, has a prodigious reputation for breakfasts;
but Cornwall, on occasion, can almost rival Yorkshire in
the matter of tea. Laddie and Lassie had set to work
already, one on each side of Miss Hawberk, who was
engaged with urn and teapot. Moppet was less intent
upon food, and had more time to wonder and scrutinize.
Her big mind was hungrier than her little body.

"Oh, what a lot of candles!" she cried. "You must
be very rich, Mr. Old Gentleman."

Eight tall candles in two heavy old silver candelabra lighted the large round table, and on the dazzling white cloth was spread such a feast as little children love— cakes of many kinds, jams, and marmalade, buns, muffins, and crisp biscuits fresh from the oven, scones both white and brown, and the pale yellow clotted cream in the preparation of which Cornwall pretends to surpass her sister Devon, as in her cider and pery and smoked pig. It is only natural that Cornwall in her stately seclusion at the end of Western England should look down upon Devonshire as sophisticated and almost cockney. Cornwall is to Devon as the real Scottish Highlands are to the Trossachs. Besides the cakes and jams and cream-bowl, there were flowers, Christmas roses, and real roses, yellow and red, such flowers as only grow in rich men's greenhouses, and there was a big silver urn in which Laddie and Lassie could see their faces, red and broad and shining, as they squeezed themselves each against one of Adela's elbows.

"Oh, Uncle Tom," exclaimed Lassie, in a rapturous tone, "we shall never die here."

" Not for want of food certainly, Lassie."

The children had eaten nothing since a very early dinner in Plymouth, and on being pressed to eat by Miss Hawberk and Mr. Danby, showed themselves frankly greedy. Sir John did nothing but look on and wonder at them. They showed him a new phase of humanity. Did life begin so soon ? Was the mind so fully awakened while the body was still so tiny ?

" How old are you, Mistress Moppet ? " he asked, when Moppet had finished her first slice of saffron cake.

" Four and a quarter."

Not five years old. She had lived in the world less than five years. She talked of what she had thought and believed when she was little ; and she seemed to know as much about life as he did, at sixty-five.

" You are a wonderful little woman, not to be afraid of going out visiting without your nurse ? "

" Nurse ? " echoed Moppet, staring at him with her big grey eyes ; " what's a nurse ? "

" She doesn't know," explained Laddie. " We never had a nurse. It's a woman like Julie has to take care of

her, Moppet," he explained condescendingly—"a *bonne*
we call her.   But we've never had a *bonne*," he added
with a superior air.

" Indeed," exclaimed Sir John; " then pray who has
taken care of you, put you to bed at night, and washed
and dressed you of a morning, taken you out for walks, or
wheeled you in a perambulator ? "

" Mother," cried the boy.   " Mother does all that—
except for me.   I dress myself.   I take my own bath.
Mother says I'm growing quite inde-in-de—— "

" Pendent," screamed Moppet across the table.   " What
a silly boy you are !   You always forget the names of
things."

Moppet was getting excited.   The small cheeks were
flushed and the big eyes were getting bigger, and Moppet
was inclined to gesticulate a good deal when she talked,
and to pat the tablecloth with two little hands to give
point to her speech.

" Moppet," said Mr. Danby, " the hot cakes are getting
into your head.   I propose an adjournment to Bedfordshire."

"No! *no!* no! Uncle Tom. We ain't to go yet, is we?" pleaded the child, snuggling close up to Sir John's waistcoat, with the settled conviction that he was the higher authority. The lapse in grammar was the momentary result of excitement. In a general way Moppet's tenses and persons were as correct as if she had been twenty.

"I think you ought to be tired after your long journey," said the baronet.

"But it wasn't a long journey. We had dinner first, and in the morning we walked on the Hoe. Isn't that a funny name for a place? And we saw the sea, and Uncle Tom told us of the—— "

"Spanish Arcadia," interrupted Laddie, who felt it was his turn now, "and how Drake and the other captains were playing bowls on the Hoe, just where we were standing that very minute, when the news of the Spanish ships came and they went off to meet them; and there was a storm, and there was no fighting wanted, for the storm smashed all the ships, and they went back to King Philip without any masts, and Queen Elizabeth went on horseback to Tilbury, and that was the end of the Arcadia."

"For a historical synopsis I don't call that bad," said Mr. Danby ; "nevertheless I recommend Bedfordshire if our little friends have finished their tea."

" I have," said Lassie, with a contented yawn.

Moppet did not want to go to bed.   She had eaten less than the other two, but she had talked more, and had slapped the table, and had made faces, while Lassie and Laddie had been models of good manners.

" I wish you wouldn't call it Bedfordshire," she said, shaking her head vindictively at Mr. Danby.   " It makes it worse to go to bed when people make jokes about it ! "

Mr. Danby came round to where she sat, and took her up in his arms as if she had been a big doll instead of a small child.

" Say good night to Sir John," he said.

Moppet stooped her face down to the baronet's, and pursed up her red lips in the prettiest little kiss, which was returned quite heartily.

" Take her away, Danby, she is much too excited, and

she is the funniest little thing I ever saw. Good night, my dears," he said to the others, as he rose and walked towards the door. " I hope you will spend a happy Christmas at Place. Adela, be sure the little things are comfortable, and that Nurse Danby's instructions are obeyed."

The children laughed at this rude mention of Mr. Danby, and went off to bed repeating the phrase " Nurse Danby " with much chuckling and giggling.

CHAPTER IV.

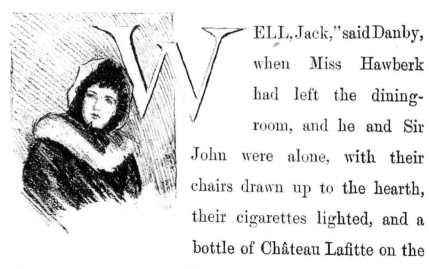

"WELL, Jack," said Danby, when Miss Hawberk had left the dining-room, and he and Sir John were alone, with their chairs drawn up to the hearth, their cigarettes lighted, and a bottle of Château Lafitte on the table between them. "Have you forgiven the children for being so much smaller than you expected?"

"I could forgive that youngest mite anything—smashing the Portland vase, if I owned it. She is what your friends over yonder" (with a nod westward) "would call an amusing little cuss."

"She is a little lump of love," answered Danby. "One has to know that child well to know how much there is in her."

"You are very weak about her evidently—very fond of all three, no doubt?"

"Yes, I am fond of them all. Lassie is going to grow up a beauty. I shall be very proud of her twelve years hence, if I live so long."

"You say they are not actually your nephew and nieces?"

"Not actually!"

"But they are pretty nearly related to you, I take it?"

"They are as near to my heart as they can be!"

"You are not very explicit."

"Why, no, Jack; that isn't in the bond. It was agreed that the children were to come and go, and you were to know nothing about them, except that they were decently brought up, and not likely to make themselves obnoxious. They were to have no claim upon you. This visit was not to be the thin end of the wedge."

"You needn't echo me, Danby. I dare say I was rather cantankerous the other day."

"No, no, Jack, you were open-handed and liberal, as you always are; but naturally you didn't want, by a casual kindness, to establish a claim, or to give anybody's poor relations the right to bother you. We'll stick to the original notion, my dear friend. These children are hired to amuse you, and to give just the touch of homely mirthfulness that suits the season. They will enjoy all the good things your hospitality provides, and their frank happiness will enliven this solitary old house, and on the morning after Twelfth Night they will wish you good-bye, and will be seen no more at Penlyon Place."

"Manage it your own way," said Sir John, with a faint sigh.

He was thinking of his daughter Lilian, his elder daughter, who had never disobeyed him—whose marriage had gratified his pride as a father. If she had lived to be a mother how happy he would have been to see the third generation growing up about him, to have

welcomed sturdy grandsons and blooming granddaughters
to the house of his forefathers, to have seen the line of
the Penlyons carried on towards the dim future, with the
promise of new honours and increasing wealth.

The bell rang at half-past eight for morning prayers,
a big bell in a cupola over the hall door. Sir John was
in his armchair near the hearth, with the large crimson-
bound prayer-book open on the table in front of him,
waiting for the assembling of the household. The bell
was still ringing when a scampering of little feet was
heard in the hall, the door was opened rather violently,
and Laddie and the two little girls came rushing in, their
eyes sparkling, their cheeks fresh and cold from the
morning air.

Moppet ran straight to Sir John, and lifted up her
rosebud mouth for a kiss, and was immediately taken
upon his knee. It seemed the only possible thing to do
with such a small creature, so round, so caressing, so
bright and fresh with sweet morning breezes and morning
sunshine.

"What a veway nice garden yours is," said Moppet, approvingly.

"You have seen the garden already. What an early bird you are!"

"Yes, but I didn't catch any worms. I don't like worms. They're veway ugly," said Moppet, shaking her head. "I'm not afraid of them *now*, not even when they're ever so big; but I—do—not—like—them."

She slapped her open palm upon Sir John's coat-sleeve to give emphasis to this final statement: such a tiny, tiny hand, but with so much character in all its movements. Laddie and Lassie meanwhile were walking slowly round the breakfast-table, looking at the good things upon it. The big Cornish ham and savoury pie, and cold pheasants were on the sideboard; but the large round table was amply furnished with covered silver dishes, in which the children admired themselves, and crystal jars of jam, and bowls of clotted cream, just the same as at last night's tea.

Laddie came to a full stop, gazing with wide open eyes, and gave a long sigh of content.

"Poor mother!" he said, almost in tears.

"What's the matter with mother?" asked Moppet from her perch on Sir John's knee.

"She never has breakfast like this."

"She has what she likes. Mother isn't greedy like you. Cake doesn't make her happy, nor even jam," said Moppet, with a philosophical air. "She has an egg every morning. My fowl lays it for her, sometimes."

"So you keep fowls, Moppet?" asked Sir John, curiously interested in every detail of these small lives.

"I keep a fowl—a hen; cocks are ever so much prettier, but they are fierce, and they won't lay eggs. I have got a hen, and she has got one, and he has got one," said Moppet, pointing to the brother and sister, "and they all lay eggs for mother's breakfast, except when they won't."

"Hush, my pet, I am going to read prayers."

"Are you?" said Moppet, looking at him with wondering eyes. "Why don't you say your prayers dreckly you're dressed, like we do?"

"These are family prayers, for everybody."

"Oh," said Moppet, resignedly, with a very long face, "like church, I s'pose."

Adela Hawberk and Mr. Danby came in one by one during this conversation, and Adela now took Moppet, as it were, into custody, while Danby looked after the other two. The three children were seated solemnly, with their little hands quietly folded, but their eyes roaming about the room, when the servants came filing in, and took their places near the door—the butler, portly and pompous; the valet, tall and slim, languidly elegant; the cook colossal; the maids fresh-coloured and prim, in cotton frocks and smart white caps; and Miss Hawberk's woman, bringing up the rear, in a neat black gown and a something of lace and ribbon, which was as little like a cap as she could make it.

Moppet, with her mouth ·wide open, counted these good people in a loud whisper, and then, just as Sir John opened his book, and began the preliminary scriptures, turned to Miss Hawberk in irrepressible surprise, and exclaimed aloud—

"Twelve servants! Mother has only one!"

She looked very sorry the next instant, when she heard her little clear voice clash against Sir John's deep tones, and till the very end of the family prayers she knelt or sat as mute as a statue.

The prayers were not too long for any one's patience. The servants filed out of the room as quietly as they had entered, Miss Hawberk's Abigail departing with an indolent grace, and with the door held open for her by an admiring footman. Then came a delicious odour of coffee; and then the business of breakfast began in earnest, and the children, who had been up at the first glimpse of day, eager to find the toys in their stockings, "mother's" little gifts among them, and who had been dressed and running about since half-past seven, were quite ready for the meal. Mr. Danby looked after them, and took care that they had only the things that were good for them, and those composed a somewhat Spartan bill of fare.

The butler, who was on duty at the sideboard, carving, approached Laddie as solemnly as if he were a grown-up person, and offered him a plate of pheasant and ham. Laddie looked appealingly at Uncle Tom.

"Not to be thought of, Laddie! You are going to have a dinner fit for a Lord Mayor of London, and you must save yourself for that. Bread and butter and an egg for breakfast, and nothing more."

Moppet, who was breakfasting on a basin of bread and milk, shook her head at her brother across the wide, round table.

"You know, Laddie, we never have meat for breakfast," she said, "and we don't always have it for dinner. Sometimes we have rice pudding, and sometimes we have batter pudding," she explained to the company in general; "and then we don't want meat, you know. It's better for us, and it's cheaper for mother."

She was as much at home in the dining-room at Penlyon Place as if she had been in her own nursery. She had dragged a chair close to Sir John's elbow, and had placed herself at his side unbidden. Moppet had a preference for the ruder sex, perhaps resulting from her experience of her good friend Danby, who indulged her more than anybody else in her small world. She admired Adela, and she liked Adela's frock, and the way her hair was done; but she wanted to sit next the nice old gentleman with the black eyebrows and silver-grey hair, who had taken her on his knee and talked to her in his big, deep voice.

The church was close to the gates of Penlyon Place, and they all walked there together on this fine Christmas morning. It was what people call a green Christmas, the air soft and warm, the sky blue, and the sun shining on the leafless branches of oak and beech and on the green underwood.

"There ought to be snow at Christmas," said Lassie. "It isn't like Christmas without snowballing."

The children behaved so discreetly in church that it was clear that they were good little church people, and that the service was familiar to them, though only Laddie made any pretence at reading his Prayer-book, and he always read in the wrong place. Never a word spoke Moppet all through the long rustic service, though her eyes and her sensitive lips were eloquent of many emotions—wonder at the monuments on the wall in front of her, the knightly gentleman kneeling face to face with his stately lady, and a diminishing line of six kneeling boys behind him, and a diminishing line of six kneeling girls behind her.

"Had they really six apiece?" Moppet asked Sir John, as she trotted homeward by his side, her tiny hand held firmly in his strong fingers.

"Six what—who?"

"Had the gentleman with the frill round his neck six little boys? and had the lady with the frill round her neck six little girls?"

"Yes, Moppet, it's quite true, only they shared them."

"Then why are the boys all on one side?"

"I suppose it's a more orderly arrangement."

"Were they all dead—down to the very littlest boy when that thing was made?"

"I hope not, for it would give me a poor opinion of Cornwall as a health resort two hundred and fifty years ago."

"Was it as long ago as that when there were those little boys?" asked Moppet.

"Longer. Nearly three hundred years!"

"Three hundred! What a pity! I should like to have six little boys like those to play with!"

"What would you do with them?"

"Lots of things. We could play at battles—one can't make a battle with three. It isn't like it."

"And it isn't a fair fight either, Moppet, two to one."

"No, but Laddie thumps very hard. We have to push him down and sit upon him; and when he can't get up we've won!" explained Moppet, with a triumphant air.

Lassie had been walking ahead with Adela, but she came running back and placed herself on Sir John's other side, pushing a very small hand, but not so tiny as Moppet's, into his.

"I hope you like me a little bit, too," she said with dignity.

"Of course I do, Lassie. I think you are a very nice little girl."

"But you don't like me as well as you do her," pointing to Moppet.

"Perhaps I know her best. She is such a forward young lady, and she and I are quite old friends."

"Not really older than me and you," said Lassie.

"Is it naughty to be forward?" Moppet asked gravely, having considered the phrase.

"Not at four years old. You won't be able to jump upon an elderly gentleman's knee and put your arms round his neck when you're four and twenty."

"I shall be too big; and I shouldn't want to unless I liked him as much as I like you. Little girls sit on their father's knees, don't they?"

"Sometimes."

"I mean good little girls. And that isn't being forward, is it?"

"No, Moppet, no. Fathers are made to be sat upon!"

"I wish you would be my father."

"Why, Moppet?"

"Because I never had one. Never, never. It's

curious, isn't it? Other little girls say it's curious when I tell them about it. Mother's a "—stopping with a puzzled look—" the kind of person who has a dead husband."

"A widow," suggested Sir John, startled at the turn of speech.

"Yes, a widow. And I was born after he was dead. It's so long ago that I don't remember, and mother was very sorry then, awfully sorry, and she was so ill and so sorry that she didn't care about me. She didn't even know I was there. It was months and months before she knew anything about me; but, when she began to know, she liked me very much, and that's why I'm her favourite child," explained Moppet.

"You mustn't talk about favourites. A mother loves all her children alike."

"That isn't true," said Moppet. "But you're not a mother, and you don't know, so you didn't mean to tell a story."

Sir John accepted this rebuke meekly, and as they had now arrived at the hall door he informed his young friend that he had some letters to write, and must part company with her for an hour or two.

The little woman in red looked up at him with a sorrowful face. She was an adhesive young person, and she had taken a fancy to her host.

"Mayn't I come with you?" she asked plaintively. "I'll be very quiet. I sit with mother when she writes her letters, and sometimes she lets me wipe the pen. She has such a dear little penholder, like a tortoise-shell cat, only it's not alive."

Sir John was polite but firm. He was charmed with Moppet, but he preferred to write his letters without her company.

"We shall meet at dinner," he said, stooping very low to kiss the atom of a hand.

"And I shall sit next you?" asked Moppet.

"On my right hand, as the guest of the evening."

CHAPTER V.

THE Christmas custom at Pen-lyon Place was one which in Sir John's mind reduced Christmas Day to a penitential anniversary. On Christmas Day the family dinner was at five o'clock instead of at eight, in order that the servants might enjoy their evening.

"Their evening!" echoed Sir John, ruefully, when the matter was put before him as a sacrifice which the head of a respectable British household was called upon to make. "Their evening, forsooth! As if they had not three hundred and sixty-five evenings in the year in which to take their ease and be merry from nine to eleven, but

I

must needs throw *our* lives out of gear, and make *our* evening wretched with the memory of a ridiculously early dinner, while they are uproarious over snapdragon or forfeits in the servants' hall. The whole thing is an absurdity."

Absurd as it was, Sir John had been coaxed into submission; and now on this particular Christmas Day he was quite resigned to the five-o'clock dinner, and was amused at the delight of the little hirelings, who clapped their hands and jumped and chirped like three grasshoppers.

"We're all going to have late dinner!" they cried, in a chorus of small silvery voices.

"You poor things!" exclaimed Miss Hawberk. "Do you never have late dinner at home, not even on Christmas Day?"

"Never," answered the boy. "There isn't any late dinner. Mother dines with us very early, and then in the evening, when the candles are lit, we all have tea, mother and all of us, and jam sandwiches, and then I sit by the fire and learn my spelling while mother puts Lassie and Moppet to bed."

"He stops up last because he's the oldest," explained

Moppet, who always addressed her small speeches to Sir John, "and we don't learn no spelling because we're too young. But I know most of Laddie's words," she added with sly triumph. "Laddie is very slow, and I'm rather quick."

"Too quick, Moppet," said Mr. Danby, lifting the tiny creature in his arms, and looking at her with a touch of melancholy. "If my watch were to go as fast as that small brain of yours I should be afraid the works would wear out."

The children went for a walk on the cliffs with Miss Hawberk and the gentleman whom they called Uncle Tom, and while they were strolling in the grey softness of a green Christmas, watching silvery sea-gulls wheeling and chattering in the soft grey sky, or congregating on a ledge of rocks, and the black shags diving for fish, Sir John came across the hillocky turf and joined them.

"Have you written all your letters?" asked Moppet, severely.

"As many as I cared to write, little one. The mild afternoon tempted me to a stroll."

Moppet waited for no permission, but at once possessed herself of Sir John's forefinger, and held on to his thick doeskin glove with a firm little grip. He could but wonder that such tiny fingers could hold him so tight.

"And what does Moppet think of the sea?" he asked.

"I like your sea better than our sea at home. There are such big, big, big rocks, and such a lot of black birds, and such a lot of white and grey birds. Uncle Tom showed us a rock just now that was all covered with birds. You couldn't see the rocks for the birds. And then he threw a stone and they all flew off screaming, screaming like human persons. It was so funny!"

"Then it seems you live by the sea when you are at home, Moppet?"

"Always—'cept when it's the season, and then mother lets her house to an English family, and we go to a farm where there are calves, and pigs, and ducks and chickens, and where we all wear wooden shoes and run about in the mud. It's lovely."

"So, Moppet, you are only half an English girl. You live on the other side of the Channel?" said Sir John.

"I don't know what you mean by the Channel. We live in F'ance, but we're not F'ench." The letter *r* represented difficulties not always surmounted even in Moppet's exceptionally distinct speech. "Mother's English, and father's English, and we're English."

"Your father *was* English," corrected Sir John. "You told me your father was dead."

"Ah, but we never say *was* about father. Mother likes us to think that he's always with us, though we can't see him. His spirit is there, you know, and he is glad when we are good, and he is very, very sorry when we are naughty—most of all when we are unkind to each other. Laddie didn't think of that the day he gave me the bad slap," continued Moppet, as if she were speaking of an event in history, like the Indian Mutiny, "or he wouldn't have done it; but he thought of it afterwards, and he was awfully sorry for having grieved father."

"How is it you don't all talk French, Moppet, since you live in France?"

"Because we always live with mother, and she talks English with us. She doesn't want us to learn French from servants and common people; so we only know the useful words—things you know—food and clothes and such things, and how to ask our way, or to tell people where we live, if ever we should be lost. And we pick up words sometimes. We can't help learning words on the sands when we hear the little French children who are playing there, though mother won't let us play with them. And mother is going to teach us French grammar by-and-by, when we are old enough to learn properly. But I," concluded Moppet, putting on a consequential air, "am not to learn anything for ever so long."

"What a privileged little person! But why not, pray?"

"Because I'm much too clever, Mr. Minchin said. I'm greatly in advance of my age. If I were forced or worried about lessons I might have water on the brain!"

Nothing could have surpassed Moppet's grand air as she mentioned this possibility.

"Mr. Minchin is your doctor, I suppose?"

"Yes; he's a hoppafist."

"I thought so," growled Sir John. "Nobody but a fool would have talked in that way before a dear little girl."

"No, he isn't a fool really," replied Moppet, with her most grown-up air. "He didn't know I could hear him. I was playing in the garden, and the parlour window was open, and I took my little chair under the window and sat there quietly and listened."

"That was not right, Moppet."

"So mother said when I told her. But why shouldn't I listen? It was all about me."

"Perhaps; but you weren't meant to hear it."

"I hate secrets—about *me*. I don't like doctors that whisper in corners about medicines, and next morning mother comes with a dose of something horrid, because of what the doctor said yesterday when I was playing with my doll. I call that mean of a doctor. But Mr. Minchin isn't like the horrid doctors. He only gives us globules or tablaws. Can *you* swallow tablaws without tasting them?"

"I suppose you mean tabloids. No, Moppet, I have

never tried them. The doctor hasn't attacked the gout-fiend with anything so mild. Homœopathy has never tempered the wind for this shorn lamb."

Dinner at Penlyon Place on that particular Christmas Day was a grand function. The cook had surpassed herself in the preparation of plum pudding, mince pies, creams, jellies, and junket, stimulated to effort by the thought of the children. What was the use of making tarts or jellies for Sir John's table, when the master of the house rarely touched anything of that kind, hardly looked at the best trifle or tipsy cake that could be offered to him; but there was some pleasure in cooking nice things for children, even if the children were to make themselves ill by eating too much or by mixing their puddings. Christmas came only once in the year; and no restraining consideration of health or the doctor should be allowed to spoil such a joyful season.

So the creams and jellies and junket were placed upon the dinner-table, as if it had been a ball supper, in order that the children should see them; and loud and joyous were the childish exclamations at the appearance of the feast, at the clusters of tall candles in the old silver candelabra, the old-fashioned epergne with its crystal dishes of bon-bons and sparkling fruits, crowned with a large basket-shaped dish of great purple grapes; the flowers, the dazzling white damask, and diamond cut glass. There was nothing new or modish from Venice or Bohemia, no Liberty silk or fantastic ornamentation. Sir John Penlyon's dinner-table was not in the movement. Indeed, it was arranged very much as it had been for his grandfather when the century was young.

" I never saw late dinner before," said Moppet; and then with a sigh of contentment, she exclaimed, " It's very beautiful! "

The children were dressed for dinner, and there was nothing shabbily genteel or tawdrily fine in their raiment. Laddie wore a neat little black velvet suit, and the two little girls were in white cashmere frocks, which made them look more like dolls than ever.

The crowning glory of the feast was the pudding. The room was darkened in the old-fashioned way, and the great plum pudding was brought in surrounded with flames, and all the company looked like ghosts in the blue unearthly light, a ceremony repeated all over the land on that day in houses where there were children— rather boring for the grown-ups, but such a rapturous experience for the children, especially for the smallest child, who is just a little frightened perhaps at the entrance of the demon pudding, and hysterical with delight when the first shock is over.

This pudding was saluted with a tremendous clapping of tiny hands, which sounded like the applause of an audience of fairies. The whole business was rapture, most of all when it was discovered that there were some new sixpences in the pudding. The excitement increased to fever-heat when Mr. Danby found a sixpence in his portion, and exhibited an amount of pleasure which indicated an avaricious disposition, and quite shocked Moppet.

"I suppose you'll give me your sixpence," she said, stretching out a tiny palm in his direction; "you can't want it yourself."

"Can't I?" ejaculated Mr. Danby. "I do want it very much. Sixpence is sixpence all the world over."

THE PUDDING WAS SALUTED WITH A TREMENDOUS CLAPPING OF TINY HANDS.

"But a man of your age can't want sixpence," with grave remonstrance.

"Can't he? Why, there are lots of things that six-pence will buy for a man of my age. A cigar, for instance."

"But you can't want *that* sixpence. You have always lots of money. I've seen you take out shillings—a handful of shillings—from your waistcoat pocket when you were paying for our *brioches* at the pastrycook's, or buying us toys in the Grande Rue. You can't want that sixpence."

"Not to spend, Moppet. I shall keep it for luck. I shall bore a hole in it and wear it next my heart in memory of a Christmas dinner with you—your first late dinner."

"I'm glad of that," said Moppet, greatly relieved. " I was afraid you were a miser after all."

Laddie and Lassie greeted this speech with uproarious laughter.

"A miser! Uncle Tom a miser! Why, you know he is always bringing us things. Mother has to be quite cross sometimes to prevent him spending too much money upon us," said Laddie.

"Uncle Tom gave us our silk stockings," explained

Lassie. "They're real silk; not spun silk, like most little girls have. They came in a letter from Wears and Swells. Wasn't that a funny letter? Mother told Uncle Tom he was dreadfully extravagant; but he only laughed. He is not the least little bit of a miser; not nearly such a miser as Moppet, who puts all her half-francs into a money-box that won't open, and then asks mother for sous to spend."

There was more than one sixpence in the pudding. Each of the children discovered a glittering new coin, and in Moppet's portion there were two sixpences. The stout and serious butler helping the pudding on the carving-table by the light of a single candle was suspected of treasonable practices.

If the pudding with its halo of blue flame were a glorious thing, how much more glorious was the Christmas-tree in the great Tudor hall, the Christmas-tree with innumerable tapers that were reflected in the bright armour of those dead and gone warriors whose prowess had helped to win victory at Agincourt, or whose strength had prolonged the bitter struggle at home in the Wars of the Roses. Miss Hawberk had sent round some little notes of invitation, swift and sudden as the fiery cross, and had assembled all the little ladies and

THE OLD BUTLER WAS SUSPECTED OF TREASONABLE PRACTICES.

gentlemen of the neighbourhood, the pretty fair-haired girls from the Rectory, and the children of the only two gentlefolk's families within an easy drive of Penlyon

Place, and Mr. Nicholls, the old bachelor doctor, had also been invited; perhaps in order to throw in a warning word occasionally when the revellers seemed inclined to over-eat themselves. All the little girls had long hair, combed and brushed and crinkled to perfection; and they looked rather suspiciously at Lassie and Moppet's round-cropped heads, as little Africans with their hair caked in clay might look at the children of another tribe who wore no clay.

"Have you and her had a fever?" one little girl inquired of Moppet, pointing at Lassie as she asked the question.

"No!"

"Then why was your hair cut so short?"

"That's the F'ench way," explained Moppet, gravely. "We are not F'ench, but we live in F'ance, and mother likes our hair cut in the F'ench way."

"Oh," sighed the long-haired child, relieved in mind. "It's very ugly. Gracie had her hair like that once, but then she'd had a fever. Your mother must be a funny woman."

"No she ain't," cried Moppet, firing instantly. "She

ain't half so funny as your mother." Moppet pointed to a stout lady in black velvet and a Roman sash—a stout lady with a rubicund face. "I shouldn't like my mother to be as fat as yours, or as red," said Moppet, and with this parting shot marched off and left the long-haired beautifully brushed and crinkled little girl inanely staring, shocked, but far too stupid to retort, hereditary fleshiness muffling her intellectual faculties.

Sir John Penlyon had just seated himself on the great oaken settle in the chimney corner, after somewhat languidly performing his duty as host. Moppet walked straight to him, clambered on his knee, and nestled her head in his waistcoat, gazing up at him with very much the same dumb devotion he had seen in the topaz eyes of a favourite Clumber spaniel.

"Why, Moppet, are you tired of your new little friends?" he asked kindly.

"I don't like children. They are so silly," answered Moppet, with decision. "I like you much better."

"Do you really, now? I wonder how much you like me. As well as you like junket?"

"I SHOULDN'T LIKE MY MOTHER TO BE AS FAT AS YOURS, OR AS RED."

K

"Oh, what a silly question! As if one could care for any nice thing to eat as well as one cares for a live person?"

"Couldn't one? I believe there are little boys in Boscastle who are fonder of plum pudding than of all their relations."

"They must be horrid little boys. Laddie is greedy; but he is not so greedy as that. I shouldn't like to live in the same house with him if he were."

"For fear he should turn cannibal and eat *you*?"

"What is a camomile, and does it really eat people?"

"Never mind, Moppet; there are none in our part of the world," said Sir John, hastily, feeling that he had made a *faux pas*, and might set Moppet dreaming of cannibals if he explained their nature and attributes.

He had been warned by his friend Danby that Moppet was given to dreaming at night of anything that had moved her wonder or her fear in the day, and that she would awaken from such dreams in a cold perspiration, with wild eyes and clenched hands. Her sleep had been haunted by goblins, and made hideous by men who had sold their shadows, and by wolves who were hungry for little girls in red cloaks. It had been found perilous to tell her the old familiar fairy tales which most children have been told, and from which many children have suffered in the dim early years, before the restrictions of space and climate are understood, and wolves, bears, and lions located in their own peculiar latitudes.

Sir John looked down at the little dark head which was pressed so lovingly against his waistcoat, and at the long dark lashes that veiled the deep-set eyes.

"And so you really like me?" said he.

"I really *love* you. Not so much as I love mother, but veway, veway much."

"As much as Danby—as Uncle Tom?"

"Better than Uncle Tom; but please don't tell him so. It might make him unhappy."

"I dare say it would. Uncle Tom has a jealous disposition. He might shut you up in a brazen tower."

Another *faux pas*. Moppet would be dreaming of brazen towers. Imagination, assisted by plum pudding, would run readily into tormenting visions.

Happily Moppet made no remark upon the tower. She was thinking—thinking deeply—and presently she looked up at Sir John with grave, grey eyes, and said—

" I believe I love you better than Uncle Tom, because you are a grander gentleman," she said musingly, "and because you have this beautiful big house. It is yours, isn't it—your veway, veway own ? "

" My very, very own. And so you like my house, Moppet ? And will you be sorry to go away ? "

" Oh no, because I shall be going to mother."

"Then you like your own home better than this big house ? "

" No, I don't. I should be very silly if I did. Home is a funny little house, in a funny little sloping garden on the side of a hill. Uncle Tom says it is very healthy. There is a tiny *salon*, and a tiny dining-room, and a dear little kitchen, where the *bonne à tout faire* lives, and four tiny bedrooms. It was a fisherman's cottage once, and then an English lady—an old lady—bought it, and made new rooms, and had it all made pretty, and then she died; and then Uncle Tom happened to see it, and took it for mother."

"And was my little Moppet born there?"

"No, I was born a long, long way off—up in the hills."

"What hills?"

"The north-west provinces. It's an awful long way off—but I can't tell you anything about it," added Moppet, with a solemn shake of her cropped head, "for I was born before I can remember. Laddie says we all came over the sea—but we mustn't talk to mother about that time, and Laddie's very stupid—he may have told me all wrong."

"And doesn't Lassie remember coming home in the ship?"

"She remembers a gentleman who gave her goodies."

"But not the ship?"

"No, not the ship; but she thinks there must have been a ship, for the wind blew very hard, and the gentleman went up and down as if he was in a swing. Laddie pretends to remember all the sailors' names, but I don't think he really can."

"And the only house you can remember is the house on the hill?"

"Where mother is now—yes, that's the only one, and I'm very fond of it. Are you fond of this house?"

"Yes, Moppet; one is always fond of the house in which one was born. I was born here."

Moppet looked up at him wonderingly.

"Is that very surprising?" he asked, smiling down at her.

"It seems rather surprising you should ever have been born," replied Moppet, frankly; "you are so *veuay* old."

"Yes, but one has to begin, you see, Moppet."

"It must have been a twemendously long time ago when you and Uncle Tom began."

The explosion of a cracker startled Moppet from the meditative mood. It was the signal for the rifling of the tree. The crackers—the gold and silver and sapphire and ruby and emerald crackers—were being distributed, and were exploding in every direction before Moppet could run to the tree and hold up two tiny hands, crying excitedly, "Me, me, me!"

It had been settled that the tree was not to be touched

till the visitors had finished their tea. The house-party, represented by Laddie and Lassie, had been fuming and fretting at the slowness with which cakes and buns were consumed; but now Uncle Tom, robed in a long maroon-velvet dressing-gown of Sir John's, with a black velvet cap on his head, to represent a necromancer, had given the signal, and was scattering crackers among the eager hands of dancing, leaping children, all crying, " Me, me !"

Mr. Danby had taken a good deal of trouble to disguise himself. He had made himself a long beard of white horsehair—a beard which would have done for old Father Time himself—and which reached from Mr. Danby's ears to his waist. But the children hardly looked at him and expressed no astonishment at his appearance. All they cared for was to get the crackers and the toys.

" Me, me ! Another cracker, please. Please, please give me one ! " That was the cry, varied by smaller voices saying, " Dive me a doll," " Dive me that pretty fing up dere ! " pointing to a glittering gilt watch, or to a fairy in star-spangled skirt.

But the toys on the tree were little dainty things more for ornament than use. The real toys were in a great washing basket which two men brought into the hall, staggering under it.

There were toys enough for everybody; and Mr. Danby distributed them with admirable judgment. He had even a packet for Miss Hawberk, tied with blue ribbon, out of which rolled a pair of long gloves such as young ladies love. Adela screamed at sight of the gloves, just as the children screamed at their railway engines and stone bricks.

When every child had received the most appropriate toy possible and general contentment prevailed, the basket was not even half empty. Laddie peered into its depths curiously, hugging his clockwork steam-engine under his arm—a green engine modelled upon those on the South-Western Railway, which are said to be the finest in England.

"There are lots more toys," he said to Mr. Danby, with that shrewd insinuating look which marks childish greed. "Are we going to have those?"

"No, Laddie. You have had your share. Those are for other children."

"What children?"

"You'll see, Laddie, all in good time."

Laddie thought the only good time would be a time which would give him a share in those unopened parcels.

For Moppet the necromancer had a doll—a lovely fair-haired doll, with staring blue eyes which occupied about a third of her face. Nature has endowed the expensive doll with these enormous eyes. To Moppet's lively imagination the doll, from the moment it was deposited in her arms, became a personage.

"My darling, you must have a name!" she murmured tenderly. "I shall call you Mary, after me."

She ran to Sir John with her treasure.

"Isn't she lovely?" she asked; and then, without waiting to be answered, "Her name is Mary."

His wife's name! He started ever so slightly at the sound; so familiar long ago, so strange to-day.

"Why Mary?"

"She is called after me. I am her godmother. I shall have to teach her the catechism—the catechism that Laddie has to learn."

"And so you have an *alias*. I thought your name was Moppet," said Sir John, as she seated her doll on his knee and stood leaning against him, touching and examining that divine piece of waxwork, its lace petticoats, its blue silk shoes and open-work socks—a very paragon of dolls.

"You knew my real name wasn't Moppet," she said. "Nobody was ever christened Moppet! It's only one of mother's nonsense names, like Laddie and Lassie."

"Oh, then you all have bettermost names for high days and holidays. Pray, what is Laddie's name?"

"The same as yours."

"Oh, he is John, is he?"

"Yes, John—but not Sir John. He is not a bawonight," making a great deal of the strange word which the servants had taught her, as an attribute of the grave elderly gentleman to whom she had taken so kindly. "Will he be a bawonight when he grows up?"

"That's his own look-out. I take it he will have to win his baronetcy."

"Win it?   At cards?"

"Why, what does my little Moppet know about cards?"

"Lots.   We play at spekilation with Uncle Tom, for nuts, and *vingt-et-un*, and he says that's almost as good as bac-bac-bac-ca-ra!"   She stumbled over the word, but finished it triumphantly.

"I am afraid Uncle Tom is a dangerous person to be with children."

"He is.   Mother says so.   He takes us down to the *plage* and gives us donkey rides, and I once fell off"— this with an air—"and grazed my elbow.   The blood came through the sleeve of my over-all.   Lassie has never fallen off a donkey.   Laddie has.   They generally lie down with him.   He kicks them too much.   They will bear a good deal of kicking because their skins are so thick, but Laddie overdoes it.   He is not a nice boy— not always," Moppet concluded musingly.

She liked standing quietly at Sir John's knee with her doll, though the other children were playing Post in a noisy circle round Mr. Danby and Adela on the other side of the hall. The many-coloured tapers on the Christmas-tree were all extinguished but not burnt out, only half-burnt, and the tree was still covered with golden balls, and tiny oranges, and glittering green and ruby fish, and fairy dolls nodding and trembling in space.

"Wouldn't you like to go and play with the children over there, Moppet? They seem to be having a spirited game."

"I don't care for games. I like to be here with you and Mary. You don't mind me here, do you?"

"No, my dear. I think I can put up with you till your bedtime."

That word bedtime is always a damper to juvenile spirits. In all those early years of life the idea of bed is pretty much what the idea of Portland or Dartmoor is to the criminal classes. Children hear their elders talk of wanting to go to bed, and wonder at such a perverted taste. There is always a sense of humiliation in that premature banishment. The grown-ups sit smiling and talking—bid goodnight condescendingly in a parenthesis —and one feels that their evening is only just beginning. The elder sisters step into a carriage perhaps, and are whisked off to the opera or play-house, while strong-armed Nurse conducts the little ones to their nursery cots—to premature night and darkness that seem endless. It is a cruel inequality of fortune.

"Isn't it a lovely tree?" Moppet inquired presently, her eyes wandering to that fairy-like conifer in the middle of the hall, with horizontal branches rising tier above tier, laden with things of beauty.

" Yes, it is a fine specimen of the *arbor toyensis.*"

" There's only one thing that makes me sorry about it," said Moppet, with a sigh.

" And what may that be? "

" Everybody hasn't got a tree."

"Ah, you are a little socialist. You would like all children to have just as good a Christmas as you are having."

"Why shouldn't they? They're just as good as me, ain't they? "

"I suppose they are, Moppet; only you happen to be here and they are somewhere else. But don't be down-hearted, my pet; there are a great many Christmas-trees blooming with toys and golden flowers to-night, and thousands of children dancing round them, just as happy as you and Lassie and Laddie."

"Are there more children who have a Christmas-tree than the children who haven't a Christmas-tree?" asked Moppet, after a pause, with the child's love of statistics.

"No, I'm afraid there are more of the treeless children than of the fortunate ones."

"Isn't that a pity? If it was only the naughty children who had to go without toys it wouldn't matter," argued Moppet, severely; "but I dare say there are naughty boys and girls getting toys and crackers, while there are poor good children without so much as a penny toy, only because their mothers haven't any money. Our mother isn't rich, but we've had a Christmas-tree ever since I can remember—quite two Christmases. It was only a little tree; but such a pretty little tree. Uncle

Tom sent us all the toys and ornaments and little coloured candles in a big wooden box; and we all helped mother to dress the tree. It was more fun than not knowing anything about it, and standing outside the door in the dark, and then coming in and being surprised. Our fun lasted ever so much longer, and we *were* surprised after all when we saw the tree with the candles all lighted. It wasn't a bit like the same tree."

"And you wouldn't have known the dolls if you had met them in the street?" said Sir John, smiling at her grave earnestness.

Bedtime, the inexorable summons, put an end to the conversation. The fair-haired Rectory girls and the other little people were bidding good night, and the girls were being muffled in pink and blue hoods and cloaks, while the boys struggled manfully with the sleeves of their warm overcoats.

A cold wind blew in from the vestibule when the outer door was opened—a nipping, frosty wind.

"There's a change in the weather," said Mr. Danby. "They've had snow at Brighton and at Portsmouth. I shouldn't wonder if our green Christmas were to change to a white one."

"Oh, how nice that would be!" cried Laddie, clapping his hands.

"Would you like to be snowed-up at Penlyon Place? Well, we don't often get snow in Cornwall, but perhaps we may be able to oblige you," said Sir John, gaily.

CHAPTER VI.

WHEN Moppet looked out of window next morning she looked at a white world — a world of fairy-like trees, whose interwoven branches made a brilliant lace-work that sparkled in the sun. A north-east wind was blowing under a blue, cloudless sky. It must have been snowing for a long time to cover the park and gardens with that thick white carpet; but the morning was bright and sunny, and Moppet thought the change delightful.

Pleasant news greeted her at breakfast. First a little present from mother, a soft Shetland shawl, knitted by mother's own fingers, and snowy-white like the outside world—a shawl to wrap Moppet's head and shoulders when she ran out into the garden. Lassie had one exactly like it, and Laddie had a big, thick white scarf. They had come in a post-parcel to Mr. Danby.

" Did mother know it was going to be cold ? " wondered Lassie.

" Mother's thoughts always go before things," said Moppet, gravely.

The next pleasantness was the news of a party, another children's party, which had been planned by Mr. Danby and Miss Hawberk, and which was submitted to Sir John for approval.

Would he object to their giving the cottage children a tea-party in the schoolhouse that evening, with the reversion of the Christmas-tree as the feature of the entertainment? They had plenty of toys left for distribution, plenty of Tom Smith crackers.

"Dear Tom Smith!" sighed Moppet. "What a nice man he must be! You don't object, do you?" she asked Sir John, squeezing her chair, with a high cushion upon it to bring her up to table level, a little closer to his own. "You'd like the cottage children to have some fun? They all looked so nice at church yesterday, in their pretty red cloaks."

"Sir John gave them those red cloaks," observed Miss Hawberk.

"How good of you! But you don't object, do you? They are such tidy children. I'm sure they'll be careful of their toys."

Moppet had her doll on her lap, wedged in between her pinafore and the table, and supposed to be consuming occasional spoonfuls of bread and milk.

Sir John did not object. They could have a tea-party for all the children in Cornwall if they liked, if they could get the pixies to bring them.

"What are the pixies?"

Moppet had to be told about the pixies before she
would peacefully finish her bread and milk. She rattled
her spoon against the basin in her excitement, and the
dark grey eyes seemed to grow larger as she listened.

There were occasional snow showers in the day, just
enough to maintain the freshness of that vast white
carpet which had been unrolled over the park.   The
north-east wind blew with a biting sharpness which it
rarely knows on that western coast, and swept every
cloudlet out of the bright blue sky.   The children wore
their warmest wraps when they ran out on the terrace,
which the gardeners had swept from end to end, piling
up a bank of snow on the outer side, all the length
of the broad walk, a store of material for the building
of a snow man which Mr. Danby assisted them to pile
up at the further end of the walk, out of sight of the
windows, lest he should be an eyesore.

This rugged and shapeless monster was not completed
till the children's early dinner, though they toiled
vigorously, digging out lumps of snow from the bank,

running backwards and forwards, flushed and eager, fetching and carrying for that accomplished sculptor, Uncle Tom, who desisted not from his labours till the monster towered like Milton's Lucifer, but with no more shape or likeness of humanity than a pillar post-box. The likeness was achieved presently by an old cloth cap of Uncle Tom's, a short pipe, two bits of coal for eyes, and two bits of stick for nose and mouth.

"I think he'll do now," said the sculptor, complacently.

"He's rather crooked," criticized Laddie, while the little girls stood, flushed and panting, with no feeling but admiration for this great work of art.

"Don't say that, Laddie," cried the sculptor. "Crookedness means destruction. A snow man must hold himself straight or he is doomed. You'd better bring me some more snow."

They rushed off with their spades and wooden baskets —spades and baskets that had been used on the beach by a former generation, and which had been produced from an old toy closet by Sarah, the housemaid. They brought more snow, and Uncle Tom thickened the base

THE THAW—DEATH OF THE SNOW MAN.

of the monster till he looked like a Druidic monument, and then they left him to his fate.

"He'll last now till the thaw," said Uncle Tom.

"Will the thaw spoil him?"

"Yes, when the thaw comes he will silently vanish away, like the Snark. There will be nothing left of him but a great puddle at that end of the terrace."

Uncle Tom sent the children off to get their shoes and stockings changed before dinner. He was like a nurse in his care of them.

Sir John was out shooting, tramping through snowy plantations, and the luncheon-dinner was a very noisy meal. Mr. Danby and Miss Hawberk let the children do as they liked. It was Bank Holiday, and that meant liberty for great and small, Mr. Danby said. There never was a merrier meal eaten at Place—certainly not within Adela's recollection.

"Christmas used to be so dreadfully dull in this house," said the young lady. "One felt one ought to be a little livelier because it was Christmas, and that only made one feel duller, don't you know. It was all very well for you, Mr. Danby, out shooting all day with Sir John and playing billiards in the evening, but I could only read a novel, or brood over all the Cinderellas I was missing."

Poor Adela had been sent to Penlyon Place, as into captivity, for more Christmas seasons than she could count, her mother and father declaring that it was her duty to go and amuse her uncle at that festive time, since he had always been particularly fond of her.

This idea of fondness on Sir John's part had no definite basis, but Mrs. Hawberk was in the habit of talking as if Adela were her uncle's acknowledged heiress.

" He must leave his money to somebody," she told her husband, " and why not to Adela?   After all these years of estrangement he will never take Sibyl into favour again."

" There is nothing so sure to happen as the unexpected," said Mr. Hawberk, sententiously.   " You had better not reckon Adela's chickens before they are hatched.   Your brother is not obliged to leave his money to anybody. He may leave it to a hospital, as many such old curmudgeons do."

"THE CINDERELLAS I WAS MISSING."

"You have no occasion to call my brother a curmudgeon."

"He has never given me any reason to call him anything else."

"You and he never understood each other. As for Adela, he likes having her at Place, and there can be no doubt he is very much attached to her."

The village party was quite as successful as the genteel party, and Moppet was a much more prominent personage in the schoolrooms than she had been the night before at Penlyon. Her whole heart was in this rustic entertainment. Her eyes shone like stars, her cheeks were flushed with delight. The pretty little schoolhouse, with rooms for schoolmaster attached, had been built thirty years before by Sir John, soon after he came to his own, and everything about the building was sound and neat and trim. The Christmas-tree was in the boys' schoolroom, the tea-party was in the girls' room. The children were to know nothing about that glorious tree, or that noble collection of toys for distribution, till after tea, when the lights were to be suddenly extinguished, and the door between the two schoolrooms was to be opened, and the tree was to be seen with all its fairy-like tapers burning.

It would be a thrilling moment, and Moppet's heart beat fast as she thought of the children's rapture.

"Have they never seen a tree?" she asked Adela— "never, never, never?"

"No, they have never seen one. There are so few great houses about; and there have been no children at Place for the last twenty years. These poor little things have never had any gaiety, except the rector's summer treat."

"And they couldn't have a Christmas-tree in the summer, could they?" mused Moppet. "That would be simply silly."

Moppet held office on this occasion. She was to distribute the presents, assisted by the schoolmaster, who would tell her the names of the children and advise her choice. There was to be no long-bearded necromancer this evening. Mr. Danby did not think it worth while to disguise himself, remembering how little notice the genteel children had taken of his robe or his beard, and how all their thoughts had been centred on the tree and the toy-box. These children would no doubt be even more stolid and unimpressionable.

There they were at tea, solemnly munching, solemnly handing in their mugs for more of the steaming brew— tea ready milked and sugared in a huge urn; no nice distinctions as to sweetness or non-sweetness, no study of individual tastes: hot, sweet, milky tea for everybody. The buns were the feature of the feast. The piled-up dishes of bright yellow cake were not neglected; but the buns were first favourite. Moppet could not have believed so many buns could disappear in so short a time. It was almost as good as seeing a conjurer dispose of live rabbits. The cake dishes were half full when the meal was finished; but not a bun remained.

Suddenly there came a darkness, and one simultaneous " Oh! oh!" arose from the children, while such vulgar words as " Lawks!" and " Crikey!" floated in the steamy atmosphere. And then the door was opened, and the tree was seen, and instantly saluted by a tremendous clapping of hands and a thunder of hob-nailed boots as the children all trooped into the next room.

Oh, it was a noble tree! It looked ever so much larger here than in the great hall at Penlyon Place. The head of the fairy on the topmost branch brushed against the schoolroom ceiling as she swayed to and fro, waving a beneficent wand.

The crackers were a source of rapture, and Tom Smith was the hero of the evening. Laddie was in his element, letting off crackers all over the schoolroom with cottage boys who had never seen a cracker before, and who cried "Crikey!" or "My!" whenever one went off. Laddie did not expect another toy; but he was determined to have a good go in at the crackers. Lassie, the prim little lady, stood close against Adela Hawberk's skirt while these ruder festivities were going on, not relishing that odour of corduroy and boot leather, which is inevitable in such company. But Moppet was moving from child to child in the friendliest way, handing the toys allotted to each, explaining, patronizing, altogether mistress of the situation, a Lady Bountiful of two feet high, flushed and feverish with pleasure.

While the excitement was at its highest point Sir John appeared suddenly in the doorway. Moppet flew to him in a moment. It seemed as if he always exercised the most powerful attraction for that young person. She gravitated to him as surely as the apple falls to the ground.

"Isn't it lovely?" she asked him. "Ain't they happy? Ain't their faces red?"

"And ain't yours red, Moppet! Why, you are in a high fever. I think you had better sit on my shoulder and see the fun, instead of running about in this black hole of Calcutta."

After the sharp evening air outside, the atmosphere of the schoolroom seemed like the heat of an oven. The toys were all distributed, the box was empty, and all the dolls had been unhooked from their perches on the waving green boughs. Only the impossible golden fruits and gold and silver fish and flags remained, and the tapers were expiring in smoke.

M

Moppet sat on Sir John's shoulder surveying the crowd, each child engrossed in its own pleasure, examining its booty.

"Now, boys and girls," said the schoolmaster, "three cheers for Sir John Penlyon."

"No, no," remonstrated Sir John; "I've nothing to do with the affair."

Remonstrance was useless—the loud chorus arose about him deafeningly.

"And now for Miss Hawberk."

More cheering; loud and shrill, treble and bass.

"And now for Mr. Danby, who is always so kind to you."

More and more cheering, much louder, much shriller, as from hearts overcharged with warmest feelings.

"And now for the little girl who gave out the toys."

Another special cheer—final at least for the party from Place, for Sir John turned and fled, with Moppet sitting on his shoulder; but more cheering sounded through the winter darkness from the schoolhouse behind them as they hurried along the frosty road through the park.

"Oh, what a happy evening it has been!" said Moppet from her perch on Sir John's shoulder.

"And now you are ready for Bedfordshire," said Mr. Danby.

"No, Uncle Tom. I am not the littlest bit sleepy."

In spite of this energetic asseveration, Moppet was discovered to be fast asleep when the party arrived at Place, and in that unconscious condition was undressed and put to bed, and knew nothing more till next morning, when she awoke bright and fresh, and greatly astonished that it should be to-morrow.

CHAPTER VII.

THERE could be no doubt about Moppet's affection for Sir John Penlyon. It was not cupboard love. Self-interest had nothing to do with it. The child's young fancies centred in the grave elderly man who had so kindly and protecting an air when she nestled by his side in his roomy armchair, or squeezed herself close up against him at the breakfast or the luncheon table. Sir John would have been more or less than human had he not been flattered by this preference. She liked him better than she liked Danby; yet she had known Danby for the whole of her little life, and Danby was her slave, would crawl on all-fours for her, simulating anything zoological she might choose to order, would carry her on his shoulder for a mile on end, and studied her desires in the toy world with a reckless disregard of expense. She was fond of Danby, but not so fond as she was of Sir John.

"You're so very grand," she explained always, patting her new friend on his shoulder.

She seemed to have a precocious appreciation of this personal grandeur, for certainly Sir John Penlyon had the grand air which impresses society in general. To Moppet's fancy he absorbed into himself all the dignity of his surroundings—the portly black-coated butler, the handsome liveries and powdered heads of the footmen, the space and splendour of the house, the wide-reaching park and grounds, and those farms which stretched so far away that Moppet, asking ever so many times in a morning walk, "Are all these fields yours?" had hardly ever been answered in the negative.

"You are like the Marquis of Carabas, only it's all true instead of fibs," said Moppet.

And in her small half-conscious way Moppet admired the baronet's tall, erect figure, his handsome features, the grey hair and beard, and the strongly marked black eyebrows which gave such character to the face.

Once when some discussion as to personal beauty arose, Moppet expressed herself decisively.

"You are very pretty," she told him, "quite the prettiest of us all!"

"Would you like to be as pretty when you grow up, Moppet?" he asked.

"Of course not, you silly man. I am going to be a young lady, and wear frocks like hers," pointing to Adela's low bodice. "How funny I should look with a beard like yours!"

Sir John accepted her flatteries laughingly, and owned to Danby that the little hireling amused and interested him; but he questioned his friend no further as to her belongings. He seemed content to accept her as a waif from afar, who was to vanish out of his home as quietly as she had entered there, leaving no trace behind.

"We are to go home on the seventh day of the new year," she informed him gravely one morning, in a pause of his letter-writing.

It was her privilege—obtained by sheer persistence—to sit in his room while he wrote his letters. She pledged herself to silence and stillness, and she would sit upon her hassock in a corner by the fire, playing with her dolls for an hour at a time, without a word spoken above a whisper, so low that not a sound reached him at his writing-table; but, looking at her sometimes, he would see the little red lips moving rapidly, and he knew that an elaborate make-believe conversation was going on between Moppet and her dolls.

"Will you be glad to go away?" he asked.

"Sorry to go away, but glad to go back to mother," she answered, looking up at him with clear, truthful eyes. "Will you be sorry when I am gone?"

"I'm afraid I shall, Moppet; but I shall have to get

over it. I have had to get over worse sorrows than that."

One day Adela Hawberk came into the drawing-room excitedly, in the quiet quarter of an hour before dinner, when the children had vanished into the deep silence of Bedfordshire.

" Uncle, I have just made a discovery," she exclaimed.

" Indeed? And what may that be? "

" Moppet is the living image of the Shrimp Girl—not so pretty, but extraordinarily like."

" Have you only just found that out? "

" Only five minutes ago, coming through the gallery."

" I have seen the likeness for a long time," replied Sir John, quietly, "and I think "—with a curious emphasis— " Danby must have observed it also."

Mr. Danby blushed, but held his peace, and the butler's announcement of dinner closed the conversation.

The Shrimp Girl was a fancy portrait of Sir John Penlyon's great aunt Priscilla, by Sir Joshua Reynolds, and almost as famous as the Strawberry Girl at Summerley.

Well-informed people who were shown over Place House always made a point of asking to see the Shrimp Girl. It was a picture that had been written about by art critics, and it had been exhibited some winters ago among the old masters at Burlington House.

The little girl was painted sitting on the sands, in a reddish-brown frock, with bare head and bare feet, a shrimping net in her hand, a gipsy hat with blue ribbons lying by her side. A pretty rustic picture of a not particularly pretty child, in the painter's grandest, boldest, most supremely natural manner; and the little girl looked almost as much alive as Moppet herself.

There was a likeness, undoubtedly. The dark grey, deepset eyes, the overhanging forehead, and sensitive mouth, the dimples and mutinous smile were all suggestive of Moppet; but when the subject was reopened by Adela later in the evening, Sir John would not allow any discussion about it.

" All children of the same age and complexion are alike," he said curtly ; and Mr. Danby plunged into the conversation with an entirely new theme.

There were no more complaints about a green Christmas after that evening in the schoolhouse. The first fall of snow had been the herald of a severer winter than had been known in that western extremity of England for at least ten years.

The young people were glad and the old people were sorry. For the young there were the novel pleasures of skating and hockey on the ice ; for the old there was the fear, and in many cases the reality, of bronchitis ; and fuel was dearer, and life was harder by as many degrees as the quicksilver sank in the thermometer.

For one little person in this big busy world that wintry season seemed a time of unalloyed delight. Moppet's little red legs trotted over the hard roads and along the narrow footpaths which the gardeners had swept in park and gardens, almost always trotting beside other and older footsteps, the little red woolly hand almost always held in the warm grip of Sir John's buckskin glove, age and childhood consorting in a curious companionship.

Together Sir John and his little friend visited all the

NO MORE COMPLAINTS ABOUT A GREEN CHRISTMAS.

striking features of the neighbourhood. They stood together upon Tintagel's wind-blown height, and watched the white-breasted gulls holding their parliament on the long low lines of smooth dark rock round which the spray danced and the emerald green water tumbled so merrily. Moppet loved those bold and perilous heights.

"I should be afraid if I was here quite alone, or even with Miss Hawberk," she explained; "but I'm not a bit afraid with you;" and indeed the tenderest and most experienced of nurses could not have been more careful of a tiny charge than was Sir John Penlyon.

"Did you ever have any little girls of your own?" Moppet asked him one day.

"Yes, Moppet, once upon a time."

"And did you love them veway, veway, veway much," with intense emphasis, "ever so much better than you love me?"

"Love cannot be measured off-hand, Moppet. It is a long time since I had any little girls of my own."

"I am veway glad of that," said Moppet; and Sir John was glad that she asked no further questions.

He took her to Pentargain Bay, to see the seals, and would have been very pleased to show her those creatures had there been any on view; but as there were none visible to the naked eye he could only tell her about the ways and habits of the seal tribe: and he took her down to the beach and prowled about with her between the caves and the sea, and she was full of interest and excitement.

Playing quietly in the library next morning while Sir John wrote his letters, he saw that she had made a kind of tent of *Whitaker's Almanack*, and had put three or four old gold seals—those ponderous gold and cornelian seals of the eighteenth century—in this tent, and was contemplating them with evident satisfaction.

"What new game is that, Moppet?" he asked.

"I am playing at seals."

"But those seals are not a bit like the animals I told you about yesterday."

"I know that, only I can make believe they are nice soft hairy animals, with funny blunt noses, living on land and in water. They are *seals*, you know."

"That is a tremendous stretch for your small imagination."

Small imagination, quotha! The dark, deep-set eyes gazing up at him indicated a power of imagination rare even among men and women.

The ice on the pond in the park was pronounced to be in perfect condition one bright morning, and Adela Hawberk gave herself up to the delight of skating with a little party of genteel youths from the neighbourhood. It was an ice carnival in a small way. Hot drinks and other refreshments were sent from Place House. The villagers came to look on. Mr. Danby was in his glory cutting figures upon the ice, and taking care of the children, who had a slide in a corner, upon which they slid and tumbled untiringly, with much noise of shrill voices and happy laughter. It was nearly dark when they all went back to the house, Moppet upon Danby's shoulder. There was only time for a very noisy tea, at which Moppet's excitement and conversational powers were tremendous—before the journey to Bedfordshire.

"I hope the sea will be frozen by the time we are home with mother," said Moppet, as she was carried off.

Laddie and Lassie went back to the pond next day with Miss Hawberk; but Moppet was reported to have a cold, and was kept indoors. She did not rebel against this decree, but was quite contented to sit on her hassock in her favourite corner by Sir John's fireside, with her dolls and Christmas toys spread about her on the hearthrug.

Looking up now and then from his letters, Sir John saw that she was not as busy with her dolls as usual. She sat very quietly, with her head leaning against the marble column of the chimney-piece, and her favourite doll, the one she had christened Mary, lying in her lap.

"I'm afraid my Moppet is not very well to-day," he said.

"Oh yes, I'm very *well*, but I've got a little cold. People don't take powders for colds," she added hastily; "they only stay indoors and keep themselves warm. I am veway warm, thank you." She screwed herself still

SHE SCREWED HERSELF STILL CLOSER INTO HER SNUG CORNER
BY THE FIRE.

closer into her snug corner by the fire, and he saw her
eyelids droop heavily over the tired eyes.

Certainly Moppet was not quite herself to-day. Her
eyes were very dull, and her voice was thick ; but everybody knows that these are the common symptoms of the
common cold. Sir John would not allow himself to be
uneasy about an everyday childish ailment.

When the luncheon gong sounded she told him she
did not want any dinner, and would rather stay where
she was. He compromised the matter by ordering a tray
to be brought, and the old housemaid Sarah appeared with
roast mutton and rice pudding, and tried her best to coax
the child to eat ; but Moppet stuck to her text.

"No, thank you, Sarah; I'm sure it's very nice, but
I'd rather not have any of it till to-morrow," she said.

The day wore on to evening, the premature evening of
those dark days after Christmas, and still Moppet sat in
the corner fast asleep. Sir John had taken the velvet
pillows from his sofa, and had made a luxurious little
nest for the child in the angle of the projecting chimney-
piece—a warm nook where the fire-glow could not scorch

her face. Here she slept—breathing very heavily—till Mr. Danby came to look for her at afternoon tea-time.

The footman came in with a lamp immediately after him, and Sir John started up from his forty winks in his big armchair on the opposite side of the hearth. He had been giving himself a holiday in the dusk of the evening.

"Come, Moppet," said Mr. Danby, kneeling down beside the child. "Aren't you ready for tea? Why, what a cosy little bed you have made for yourself, and what a lazy little puss you are!"

The eyelids were lifted languidly, the dark grey eyes looked at him wearily, as if they hardly recognized the familiar face.

"I don't want any tea," said the small voice, piteously. "I want to stay here. Please go and take care of the others."

She coughed with a short dry cough that alarmed Mr. Danby's ear. He knew much more about children and their ailments than Sir John Penlyon, old bachelor though he was.

HE FELT THE LITTLE LANGUID HANDS. THEY TOO WERE SCORCHED
WITH FEVER.

"I'm afraid my Moppet is ill," he said gravely, lifting the weary little figure into a chair opposite Sir John's, where the lamplight shone full upon flushed cheeks and swollen eyelids.

He felt the little wrist. Alas! the pulse was galloping faster than any horse in Sir John's stables had ever galloped—galloping on the road that leads to wild fancies and strange delusions and all the terrors of fever.

"Good God!" cried Sir John, bending over Moppet, and thoroughly scared by this time, "the child's forehead is burning."

He felt the little languid hands. They too were scorched with fever.

"It's nothing veway bad," exclaimed Moppet. "I've often been feverish before."

But the little choking cough which interrupted even this short speech, the quick panting breath, and the vivid crimson flush gainsaid Moppet's reassuring words.

Mr. Danby took her up in his arms.

"She must go to bed this instant," he said. "You'd

better send off at once for the doctor, Jack. I'm very sorry to have brought this trouble upon you."

" I'm very sorry the child should be ill," said Sir John, ringing the bell furiously.

" Please don't be unhappy about me," gasped Moppet, as she was carried off, looking back at Sir John from the threshold, and waving a hot little hand in affectionate leave-taking. "I'm not going to be veway bad—children are so soon up and down, you know—but I'm afraid I shall have to be poulticed."

Poultices were the word. Before midnight the whole household was concerned about Moppet's poultices. The doctor had been at Place three times since tea-time, and a nurse had been telegraphed for, and was to arrive from Plymouth next morning; for Moppet was down with acute congestion of the lungs, and as the evening darkened into night, the symptomatic fever began its dreary effect upon the childish brain, and Moppet's wits were wandering in strange places, and strange visions were passing before those shining glassy eyes, which seemed to see nothing of the real people about her bed, the serious upper housemaid, who put on the poultices, or Adela Hawberk, always ready with lemonade for the thirsty lips, or the doctor bending gravely down to listen to the laborious movement of the chest, or to take the patient's temperature.

Little French phrases dropped from the dry lips now and then, and it was clear that the child fancied herself in France again. And very often there were appealing cries to mother, which smote Sir John's heart with intolerable pain, as he stood just inside the door of the spacious bedroom, hidden from Moppet by the tall four-leaved screen which sheltered the bed from the hazard of draughts.

The little life was trembling in the balance, he told himself, though the doctor had sounded no note of alarm, had indeed been quite cheerful about his small patient.

"It's rather a sharp attack," he told Sir John. "But children generally take kindly to congestion of the lungs."

"This child is so fragile—— "

"Fragile! Not a bit of it," interrupted Mr. Nicholls. "Wiry, not fragile. There's a great deal of brain, rather too much brain, perhaps. The dull child has always a better chance than the clever child. But I hope this one will do very well. It's all a question of nursing. The trained nurse will be here to-morrow morning—and in the mean time all my instructions are being carried out by Miss Hawberk and the maid."

They were thus distinctly assured that there was no danger; yet nobody at Penlyon seemed inclined to go to bed that night. One o'clock struck with the sound of ghostly solemnity which belongs particularly to the single solitary stroke of the first hour after midnight; two o'clock struck, and Sir John and Mr. Danby sat reading by the drawing-room fire, pretending not to know how late it was.

At half-past two Adela came fluttering in to tell them that Moppet was asleep; very feverish still, and still with short and painful breath, but sleeping. That was in itself cause for rejoicing.

After this hopeful news Sir John discovered the

lateness of the hour, and he and Mr. Danby bade each other good night.

"I'm very sorry the child is ill, for your sake, Danby," he said. "I know how fond you are of her."

"Yes, I could not be fonder of her; and it may be my fault that she is ill. I hate myself for having kept her so long in that east wind; but she was so happy, she was enjoying herself so thoroughly. I never dreamt of danger."

"Don't talk of danger. Nicholls says she will be better to-morrow, and if she isn't better we'll get some great man from London. But I have faith in our Boscastle doctor. He has a great deal of experience and plenty of sound common sense, and he has no antiquated notions. But we'll telegraph for a physician to-morrow morning, even though the child be better. We won't waste time," added Sir John, uneasily.

It was wonderful to see him so strongly moved by the waif's illness, he who was supposed to have outlived every gentle emotion.

He sent his telegram by a mounted messenger before

seven o'clock, a telegram addressed to Dr. South, the famous children's doctor, entreating him to travel by the express from Waterloo which would arrive at Launceston before six o'clock. A carriage would be waiting for him at the station to bring him over the moor to Penlyon.

" We'll have the highest authority," Sir John said to Mr. Danby, who came into his room just as the servant carried off the message. " We must not have to reproach ourselves with neglect, if——"

He did not finish the sentence, but bent over his writing-table to arrange the papers which he had thrust aside when he wrote his telegram.

It was not seven o'clock yet, and the master of Penlyon Place was in his dressing-gown. His valet would not come to him till eight; but sleep had been impossible, and the only relief was in moving about his room by the ghastly morning candle-light, while Danby, who was fully dressed, stood looking at him.

"Danby!" cried Sir John, presently, stopping in his slow pacing up and down; " you look as if you hadn't been in bed all night."

HE SENT HIS TELEGRAM BY A MOUNTED MESSENGER BEFORE SEVEN
O'CLOCK.

"I haven't—much."

"Danby, you're a fool—a fidgety old fool. You heard what Nicholls said about children—they generally take kindly to congestion of the lungs."

"Yes, I heard him—and I have heard her breathing. One might take kindly to a wolf sitting on one's chest, but one would rather not have him there. Take kindly! That's a doctor's phrase for struggling through a painful malady. The child survives where the adult might succumb; but in the mean time there's acute suffering to be borne somehow. And Moppet is so patient! One feels angry with Providence—for punishing—such a— little creature."

Mr. Danby escaped hurriedly from the room, but Sir John heard something like a sob before the door shut behind him.

"What fools we are!" he muttered. "All this fuss and anxiety about a child, when all the London slums are choked with children whose future maintenance is problematical! One child less or more upon this teeming earth! What difference ought that to make? A creature that has only just begun to think and to feel! Why, less than five years ago there was no such thing as Moppet; and now I believe Danby thinks the world would be empty without her."

Danby! Was it only Mr. Danby who was so foolishly anxious about that little life struggling with illness? Who was it who walked up and down the terrace in the early morning, watching for the coming of the doctor? Who was it who followed the doctor to the door of the sick-room, and waited outside in the corridor till he came out again; waited with aching heart and a sick dread of hearing bad news?

The news was bad. Mr. Nicholls found Moppet worse to-day than yesterday.

"If you would like a second opinion——" he began.

"I have telegraphed for Dr. South," Sir John answered curtly, "and have had his reply. He will be here this evening."

"Of course I can have no objection to meet a man of Dr. South's distinction."

Objection! As if this country doctor's feelings, and

WHO WAS IT WHO FOLLOWED THE DOCTOR TO THE DOOR OF THE SICK-ROOM,
AND WAITED?

O

the petty restrictions of medical etiquette, were to be studied when that little life was wavering in the balance —weighed in a balance so fine that a hair might turn it.

Oh that long, dreadful day of waiting and suspense! Mr. Nicholls came many times in the day, indeed he only drove hither and thither on hurried journeys to see his other patients, and then came back to Penlyon Place, making that his head-quarters. The child showed no signs of improvement as the day wore on. There was a hush throughout the house, almost as if death were already there; while Danby and Adela went about with pale faces, too restless and anxious for settled occupation of any kind. Their talk was all of the child, and of different cases of childish illness out of which the patient had come triumphantly. If they had ever known of fatal cases they did not mention those.

And all through the sunny morning and the short afternoon Laddie and Lassie were at play on a little lawn in front of the library, and a long way from the sick child's room, a spot whence no sound of those shrill young voices could reach her. They had one of the women servants to look after them, and to see that *they* did not catch cold; and they had their shuttlecocks and battledores, and bats and balls and hoops, from their treasury of Christmas·gifts, and were as full of life and spirits as if there were no such thing as suffering in the world. Sir John almost hated these small egotists, flushed and happy under the cloudless blue of a bright winter sky, Lassie skimming across the little lawn like a scarlet bird, Laddie skipping and bounding about like a boy on wires, never still.

Sir John looked so worried when they approached him that Mr. Danby, quick to read all his old friend's feelings, ordered their early dinner in the housekeeper's room instead of at the family luncheon-table. They were treated all through the day as if they were in disgrace, and nobody took any notice of them. Towards evening they grew fractious and fretful, and began to feel really sorry that Moppet was ill, or that things in general had become uncomfortable.

"I should like to go home to mother," said Lassie.

"I HAVE TELEGRAPHED FOR DR. SOUTH, AND HAVE HAD HIS REPLY."

"So should I," agreed Laddie. "It's no fun being here when there's only servants to play with."

THEY WERE AS FULL OF LIFE AND SPIRITS AS IF THERE WERE NO SUCH THING AS SUFFERING IN THE WORLD.

"We shan't have such nice dinners when we go home," mused the girl. "We shall have rice puddings some days, and potato soup some days; but not always fowls, and tarts, and cream, and junket, like we do here."

"Who cares?" cried the boy, with a dash of defiance.

"You care—very much!" retorted his sister, with vigorous assertion. "It is a story to say you don't. You know you're much the greediest of us. You quite *love* your dinner."

"So do you! So does everybody that is hungry; everybody except mother. She never cares. She likes us to have all the nice things, and pretends she doesn't want any."

And so, squabbling, but not unfriendly, and talking to each other through the open door between the two rooms, Laddie and Lassie dropped asleep, and their brief day was done; while to those elders below stairs, who waited for the London physician, it seemed hardly evening.

Sir John sat in the library, just where he had sat when the notion of the Christmas hirelings was first mooted, with the monthly time-table of the London and South-Western Railway open on his knee. He had looked at it a dozen times within the last hour to see how soon Dr. South could arrive.

It was night when there came that thrilling sound of carriage wheels—thrilling when every nerve is strained in expectation of some particular guest—and Sir John went out to the hall to receive the doctor. Then came the examination of the patient, and then the consultation within closed doors.

How long, how infinitely long it seemed to those who waited! Danby, Adela, and Sir John were in the drawing-room, having given up the library to the doctors. They sat with the door wide open, listening for the opening of that other door, which should announce the end of the consultation. It would be like the entrance of the jury after a trial of life and death. They were waiting for the verdict; waiting to know whether Moppet was to die.

At last the door opened, with the sonorous sound of a massive oaken door two hundred years old, and the two doctors came across to the drawing-room where Sir John stood waiting for them on the threshold.

"Well?" he asked.

Dr. South gave a faint sigh before he answered that monosyllabic question.

"The child is gravely ill," he said. "We are going to do all that can be done. Mr. Nicholls thoroughly understands the case. There has been no time lost, no measure omitted. But I cannot disguise the fact from you—the child is gravely ill."

"Mr. Nicholls told us that children generally take kindly to inflammation of the lungs."

"The generality of children. But this is a peculiar child—a child of a very excitable temperament, with a preponderancy of brain. The mind here tells against the body. Everything will be done, but——"   ,

"There is danger!" interrupted Sir John.

"Yes, there is danger. I should do very wrong not to admit that. Has the child no mother?"

Not for a moment did the physician mistake Adela Hawberk for the child's mother, though Adela might have been taken for any age between twenty and twenty-five, and thus might seem quite old enough to be the mother of Moppet. The doctor's keen eye saw at a single glance that this pretty young lady in the evening frock was not the sick child's mother. She was anxious and tearful and sympathetic; but the white despair, the agony of suspense and terror—that look of the wild animal at bay, and ready to fight for the menaced life of her young, which he knew in the mother's eye, was lacking here. This pretty young lady was bound by no such close tie as motherhood to the little creature struggling for breath in the room above.

"The little girl's mother is living," answered Mr. Danby. "Ought she to be sent for?"

"Undoubtedly. I hope she is not very far off."

That last sentence sounded like Moppet's death-warrant.

"She is in London."

"I thought she was in France," muttered Sir John, with a curious downcast look.

"I hope she is in London by this time. I telegraphed

to her yesterday. I told her the child was ill—but not dangerously ill—and that she had better come as far as Plymouth, in case of any change for the worse."

"Shall you know where to find her in Plymouth?" asked Dr. South.

"Yes; she will expect a telegram at the post-office."

"Good. Then get your message despatched as soon as you can."

"It's a pity you didn't tell her to come straight here," said Sir John.

Mr. Danby accepted the reproof in silence. Sir John led the way to the dining-room, where dinner was waiting for the traveller from London and the household doctor.

Dr. South was to spend the night at Penlyon, and was to be driven to Launceston next morning in time for the earliest train. There would doubtless be a change in the patient by the morning, either for better or worse. If the change were for worse, it would most likely be the last change of all, and the mother would arrive too late to clasp her living child even in a farewell embrace.

"Danby!" exclaimed Sir John, severely, when he and

his old friend had gone back to the library, "in God's name why did not you tell the mother to come straight through as fast as rail and coach could bring her?"

"I did not like," faltered Danby. "I had no right to summon her to this house without your permission."

"You might have asked my permission."

"No, no, no!" exclaimed Danby, agitatedly. "I wanted it to be spontaneous. I could not introduce the subject——"

"Pshaw! what matters it to me who comes or goes while that child is lying at death's door?" cried Sir John, fiercely. "I should not see—the person. It is of the child I think—the child only. She was calling her mother to-day when I was in the room—so sweet, so loving, so sensible. She kissed me again and again with her feverish lips as I bent over her bed. She knew me perfectly. Yet there was a touch of delirium; and she called to her mother as if she were in the room. That made my heart ache, Danby."

"Well, the mother will be here to-morrow, I hope. I telegraphed to her yesterday. After Nicholls had seen the child for the second time, I fancied he was a little uneasy about her, though he wouldn't own it. So I just walked into Boscastle and telegraphed to—the mother. She would be quick to take alarm, I dare say—though I only told her that her youngest was laid up with a severe cold, and she could come to Plymouth if she felt anxious, so as to be within easy reach. I had a reply a few hours after to say she was leaving for Folkestone by the boat. She is at Plymouth by this time, I have no doubt."

" Folkestone ! " muttered Sir John. " Then the place those children talk about is Boulogne."

" Yes, it is Boulogne—a very good place, too, for a widow with a small family. They can live as cheaply there as anywhere, and in fine fresh air."

Sir John made no comment upon this, but sat absorbed and silent by the neglected fire, and then rose restlessly, walked about the room, took a book from the shelves, taking pains to find a particular volume, opened, glanced at it, and threw it aside. His face had a look of listening, and often in his pacing to and fro he stopped to open the door, and stood for a few moments holding it ajar, as if waiting for some one.

They had moved Moppet to one of the principal bed-rooms at the top of the grand staircase, the spacious chamber in which the most important guests had been always installed when there was a house party at Penlyon. This state room had been aired and warmed and prepared in hot haste for the tiny visitor, when it was found that Moppet's bad cold was going to be a serious illness. It was chosen as the largest, airiest room in the large, airy house, and Mr. Nicholls highly approved the arrange-ment, though he had not advised it. Laddie and Lassie had their two rooms all to themselves, and—light-hearted and forgetful as they were in their morning play—in the silence and solitude of the after-bedtime affection pre-vailed over egotism, and Lassie and Laddie each shed a few tears for their missing sister.

"Do you think she'll be quite well to-morrow?" ques-tioned Lassie, sitting up in bed, and calling to her unseen brother in the adjoining room.

"I am afraid not. Sarah says she's very bad, and that

when Sarah's little niece had the same complaint she died; but then Sarah's little niece had a neglectful mother, Sarah says."

"Moppet has no mother at all now," said Lassie, dolefully. "Oh, I wish mother was here! I wish we were all at home. I don't want Moppet to die. What will mother do if Moppet dies, and she has only us?"

"She'd be very miserable with only us," replied Laddie, with a voice that was muffled by distance and bedclothes, and perhaps a little by sleepiness. "We're so big, and mother's so fond of little children."

"We must be very, very, very good, and very, very, very kind to mother if Moppet should die," Lassie said conclusively. And then, after a pause, she inquired, "Should we have to go into mourning?"

"You would, of course, because you're a girl. But I shouldn't. There's no such thing as boy's mourning, stupid," replied Laddie, awakened by what he considered a futile question. "Fancy a boy playing football in mourning—or cricket! But Moppet isn't going to die. There's a doctor from London come to cure her. Sarah said his— What is it they give doctors?" questioned Laddie, suddenly at fault. "His free—that's it! Sarah said his free would be two hundred guineas—down on the nail. I heard her tell the other housemaid so."

"What does 'down on the nail' mean?" asked Lassie, more interested in that mysterious phrase than in the coming of the medical Alcides.

Unable to explain, and really sleepy, Laddie pretended to be actually asleep. He threw a little extra power into his breathing, and the imitation soon became reality.

The night wore on—another night on which people pretended to forget the hour, and no one thought of going to bed. It was felt that Dr. South's presence in the house was a tower of strength, a rock of defence against the Great Enemy. Indeed, Sir John had reason to think so, when, stealing with cautious footfall to Moppet's room in the dead of night, he saw the physician sitting at the bottom of the bed watching for the result of his treatment.

Dr. South came down to the drawing-room half an hour

afterwards, and found Sir John and his friend sitting forlornly, far apart, like people who had nothing to say to each other. It was between three and four o'clock. The clusters of candles on the mantelpiece had burnt down to the sockets, and one of the lamps had gone out. Adela had been sent off to bed an hour before, very reluctant to go, and indeed had been met by the doctor in the corridor, in her dressing-gown, hanging about for news of the child.

"Oh, Doctor South, you don't think she's going to die, do you?" she asked piteously.

"I think we're trying very hard to save her, my dear young lady, and with God's help we may prevail," answered the doctor, gravely; and with this assurance Adela was fain to be content.

Those clinging arms, and the showers of kisses that were like the bubbling up of childish love from a deep fountain of tenderness; those bright eyes and dimpling smiles, had endeared the little hireling to the light-hearted young woman as well as to the worn-out elderly man.

The night wore on. It was five o'clock before the doctor would go to the room that had been prepared for him, and where the fire had been made up again and again by the housemaid, who sat up all night to wait upon the sick-room. Mr. Danby had to remind him of his long journey to-morrow—actually to-day—after his long journey of to-day—actually yesterday; but Dr. South made light of the matter. He could always sleep in the train. He made his final visit to Moppet's bedside at five, and went to bed, leaving instructions that he should be called instantly if there were any change for the worse.

This night—with the knowledge of danger staring them full in the face—neither Sir John nor Danby went to bed at all.

"Danby," Sir John said vehemently, stopping suddenly in front of the despondent figure seated far away from the neglected fire, "you had no right to do this thing."

"What thing?" Danby asked, looking up at him confusedly.

"You had no right to bring that little child here—and

let me love her—let her grow into an old man's heart. Think what sorrow you have made for me—a sorrow at the end of my life—if she is to die."

"She shan't die," cried Danby. "We're making a good fight of it anyhow. I tell you she shan't die," he repeated huskily. "I'm going upstairs now—just to listen at her door—I won't go in. I won't risk waking her with the opening of the door. But I may hear something. The nurse may be stirring, or the maids may be in the corridor. It is agonizing to sit here, and not know if things are going well or ill."

Mr. Danby went out like a ghost, and Sir John waited in the hall while his slow soft steps ascended the stairs. He came down again in about a quarter of an hour. He had seen one of the maids, who told him Moppet was a little less restless than she had been earlier in the night.

He and Sir John made the most of this news, and at the first glimmer of the grey cold day they both went to their dressing-rooms to make bath and toilet serve instead of sleep.

Breakfast was to be at half-past eight for Dr. South,

"DANBY, YOU HAD NO RIGHT TO DO THIS THING."

who was to leave Penlyon at nine. Sir John met Lassie
on his way to the breakfast-room, very neat and prim in
her warm serge frock, quite the elder sister. Lassie was
to be six in May, a fact of which she informed people
gravely, as if she were coming into a fortune at that date.
Six years old! It is not every little girl who is soon
going to be six. Poor little things who are only four
look towards that dignified age across a desert of inter-
vening years. Lassie had learnt to tie her petticoat
strings, and put on her stockings, and even to button
her boots, in anticipation of her approaching dignity.

"Mother says I must be very useful when I am six,"
she told her friends.

Lassie ran to Sir John and put her hand into his,
looking up at him piteously.

"Mayn't we have breakfast with you, as we used to
before Moppet was ill?" she asked. "Please don't send
Laddie and me to the housekeeper's room. We haven't
been naughty, have we, Sir John?"

"No, no, my dear. You and Laddie are very good
children—only——"

He stopped with a troubled air, looking down at the small face that looked so imploringly up at his, as if he were Providence personified.

He could not tell her that, while Moppet's little life trembled in the balance, she and her brother were almost hateful to him. If Moppet were to die he would prefer the world to be altogether empty of children.

The voices and the faces of children would torture him with bitterest memories and regrets.

"You may come to breakfast with us, Lassie; but you and your brother must be very quiet. We are all of us anxious and a little unhappy about your sister."

"But she will get well, won't she?" Lassie asked, with a touch of deep distress.

"We hope so, my dear."

Laddie was skipping about in front of the great hall window, keenly interested in a solitary fly that was buzzing drowsily and knocking itself feebly against the glass. Laddie came bounding across to Sir John presently, and said—

"Please mayn't we have breakfast with you, we had no cream yesterday morning, how's Moppet?" all in a breath.

Sir John frowned upon him darkly and did not answer; but Laddie, seeing his sister go to the breakfast-room hand in hand with their host, skipped airily after them, asking no further questions. Adela came down early in her very plainest tailor-made gown, but with her hair dressed as elaborately as usual. Harrop, the maid, would hardly have neglected that beautiful auburn hair in the midst of direst calamity. Laddie and Lassie nestled on either side of the young lady, and soon began to prattle to her, and to each other across her, in low voices which grew louder by degrees.

"If you talk so loud you will be sent away," Adela murmured warningly.

"But why mustn't we talk? Moppet can't hear us upstairs in that big, big room. It's like being in church. Is it always like this when people are ill?" interrogated Laddie.

"When people are feeling unhappy they like to be very quiet."

"People who are unhappy don't like anything. Unhappiness is disliking," argued the boy, with the air of an infant Socrates.

"Are you unhappy?" asked Lassie.

"I am very anxious."

"Then you think she will die?" urged Lassie, searchingly.

"No, no, no. You must not say such things. Pray be quiet, children. Dr. South is just going."

There was a little movement and talk and a quiet leave-taking. Sir John and Mr. Danby both went to the hall door to see the physician drive away. He had done or advised all that science could do for the little girl who was fighting so bitter a battle, and he left them not utterly hopeless.

"The outlook is brighter to-day than it was last night," he said finally; "but I mustn't promise too much. We are not out of the wood yet. Please let me have an occasional telegram to say how she is going on. She is a dear little child—a most winning little child. I have seen the loveliest children who did not interest me half so much as that quaint little face of hers, with the large forehead and the dark deep-set eyes. I hope her mother will be here to-day."

Sir John did not respond to that last speech, and Dr. South stepped into the useful station brougham and was driven away by the useful upstanding horses. It is a good day's work for any pair of horses to post from Penlyon Place to Launceston and back again.

The day wore on towards evening without any marked change in the sick-room. Moppet was living and suffering; and Dr. Nicholls and the nurse were carrying out Dr. South's thoughtful treatment with the utmost care. All that science and forethought could do for the child was being done, as Mr. Danby remarked at least a dozen times in the course of the day.

He was walking with Sir John on the terrace early in the afternoon when the carriage that had taken Dr. South to Launceston drove up to the hall door. The coachman had been ordered to watch the arrival of trains for a strange lady who was to come from Plymouth, and to bring that strange lady to Place. Mr. Danby had given the man his instructions as to the style and appearance of the lady for whom he was to look out.

The bell rang, the carriage door was opened, and a lady alighted, a tall slim figure in a dark cloak, a pale face under a neat black bonnet.

Mr. Danby stood hesitatingly as she went quickly up the steps, he and Sir John being distant from the door by about twenty yards.

"Aren't you going to her?" asked Sir John, sternly.

"I—yes—of course—yes. But won't you see her—before she goes to the child?"

"See her? No!" with his darkest frown. "Why should I see her? She comes here to see her child—for that and for that alone. Go and look after her, Danby. You must consider her your guest."

Danby gave him a distressed look, and was hurrying off, when he stopped suddenly and went back to Sir John, fumbling in his waistcoat pocket as he drew near.

"Stay," he said agitatedly, "there is something I ought to have thought of before that lady entered your house." Taking a folded paper out of his letter-case, "Your cheque. There it is; and it has never left my pocket since you gave it to me. The hiring was a fiction

SHE WENT QUICKLY UP THE STEPS.

—I wanted you to know those children—and I planned the thing on the spur of the moment."

"You wanted to break my heart," said Sir John, "and it's quite likely that you will realize your wish."

"No, no. I wanted to prove to you that you have a heart."

"Go and look after your friend!"

Mr. Danby went one way, Sir John the other, and the cheque to bearer for one hundred guineas was torn up and scattered upon the thin cold air.

Deep and deeper into the heart of the park, where the wind-blown oaks all leant away from the west, went Sir John Penlyon, full of grief and anger—grief for the child who might die, anger against the friend who had brought her there.

"The meddling, officious fool! I was happy enough. I had got over the wrench that I felt when that shameless girl disobeyed me. My life was barren, but it was peaceful. What more did I want?"

What did he want now? Only the little clinging arms round his neck, the soft little cheek pressed against his own, the silvery little voice prattling gaily to him—inquiring, philosophizing, laying down the law, as if the four-year life were full to the brim of wisdom and experience. He wanted Moppet. He cared nothing for the tall young woman whom he had seen pass hurriedly under that dignified portal which she was never to have passed again.   His affection had concentrated itself upon this morsel of humanity, brought into his house by a trick—a ridiculous trick of this interfering wretch Danby.

Moppet's mother was sitting by her bedside. Moppet was better already.   Only the sight of the familiar face, only the touch of the motherly hands, had done her good.   This was the account which Adela gave Sir John when he went back to the house after dark.

"The mother seems quite a nice person," said Adela. "She has very sweet manners, and must have been very pretty, but of course her every thought is devoted to that dear little thing. There has been no time for talk of any kind. She won't come down to dinner. Mr. Danby has arranged that she shall have the dressing-room opening out of Moppet's room to sit in, and the bedroom next to Moppet's to sleep in. We shan't see her down here yet awhile."

"So much the better," said her uncle, curtly.

"Oh, I can quite understand what a bore it must be to you to have a perfect stranger brought into your house," said Adela, with a sympathetic air.

The days wore on, and Sir John saw nothing of the stranger. Nor did he see Moppet. Mr. Nicholls advised that the child should be kept as quiet as possible. There should be no one in her room but her mother and the nurse. The sensitive brain needed repose, after the long nights of fever and delirium. Moppet was improving; that was the grand point. "We have turned the corner," Mr. Nicholls announced delightedly on the third day after the mother's arrival. "We have fought a hard fight, and we are going to win."

The upstair maidservants were almost hysterical with gladness when the news was passed along the corridor and in and out of the rooms where neat housemaids in pink cotton frocks were sweeping and bed-making. Mr. Danby went about the house with a step as light as Mercury's; and everybody began to be kind to Laddie and Lassie, who had suffered a season of snubbing, and had been made to feel that nobody wanted them; except just in that ten minutes at bedtime, when their mother came to their room, and heard them say their prayers, and hung over their beds, with innumerable good-night kisses.

"May we go and see Moppet? May we play with her again?" asked Lassie.

"Not quite yet, Lassie. She will have to eat a few more dinners first."

"She won't mind that," said Laddie: "she is very fond of dinner."

"She doesn't love it as you do," remonstrated Lassie.

Sir John Penlyon left for Plymouth directly after the doctor's cheering announcement. He had business in Plymouth, he told Mr. Danby.

"Is the mother to leave Place now that the child is out of danger?" asked Danby, while his friend was waiting for the carriage.

"You and the mother can please yourselves about that," Sir John answered coldly. "I shall be away for

Q

some days.   I have to see Barton," his Plymouth solicitor.
" And I may go on to town."

" Then she had better stay till the child is well
enough for them all to go home together," Danby said
quietly.

Sir John winced as if something had hurt him.   Yes,
the child would vanish out of his life—just as she had
entered it—unless—unless he should bring his mind to
forget the wrong done him by the daughter he had
loved ; forget his stern resolve never to forgive her
or to hold communion with her after that one rebellious
act.

His daughter had taken her own course without regard
for his wishes.   She had chosen the degradation of what
to his mind was a low marriage—a marriage with a man
whose father kept a small, shabby shop in a small, shabby
street : a self-made young man, who had climbed out of
the petty tradesman's sphere by the rugged, narrow path
of patronage and help from his superiors—helped to eke
out the scholarship upon which he tried to maintain
himself at one of the least-distinguished colleges in

Oxford—a dependent at the beginning of his career, a pauper when he married.

Sir John had remembered how, in the heyday of his youth, he had crushed down and conquered his love for a girl of humble origin—how, adoring her, he had yielded to his father's sentence that for him such a marriage could never be—that the future head of the Penlyon family had duties and obligations, which must go before the romantic love of youth. He had bowed to that decree, and he had sacrificed the happiness of his early manhood. The landed gentry of Cornwall are a proud race. The roots of their family trees go down into the dark night of British history, when Mark was king and Tintagel was a place of royal revelry.

Old as Sir John was, and in spite of the progress that Liberal opinion had made since Bossiny was disfranchised, he still believed in the obligations which his ancient race had imposed upon him; and when his daughter married the grocer's son, he had told himself that he would never forgive her.

During the five years that followed her marriage he

held no communication with her, direct or indirect, knew nothing of her whereabouts. Letters, pleading passionately for pardon, came to him one after another in the first year of her married life; but they were torn and flung into the waste-paper basket, unread, and by and by they ceased to come.

A paragraph in a Plymouth paper told him of her husband's death in a remote province of Upper India, where he had been working as a missionary under the S.P.G. He had died of consumption, leaving a widow and two children.

Sir John sent the paragraph to his family solicitor, and requested him to communicate with Mrs. Morland, and to arrange for the payment of an annuity of two hundred and fifty pounds, on the understanding that she was never to molest her father either by letter or otherwise. He was to hear nothing and know nothing about her, except that the quarterly allowance was paid.

And this was all he had ever known until Danby's folly had brought her children beside his hearth, and had betrayed him into loving his unforgiven daughter's child. Gradually, slowly, the secret of the children's identity had been revealed to him. Little looks and words of Danby's, Moppet's unmistakable likeness to the Reynolds picture, the fact of their Indian birth—one thing after another had brought about the revelation, and he knew that the innocent little creature who had clambered on to his knee and clung about his neck was Sibyl Morland's child. Well, the situation had been cleverly brought about by his friend Danby; but Danby's treachery should make no difference. He might be tricked into loving his granddaughter; but he would not be tricked into forgiving his daughter.

So soon as Moppet should be well and strong again, mother and children would have to leave Penlyon Place; and in the mean time it was far better that he should be away. There must be no opportunity for surprises—no chance meetings between father and daughter.

Sir John saw his Plymouth solicitor, signed a lease, spent a night at the Grand Hotel, smoked a morning cigar on the Hoe, and went to London by the afternoon express. He stayed at a sleepy family hotel in Albemarle

Street which the Penlyons had patronized for over a century, and he bored himself exceedingly next day at the Old Masters, where every Reynolds, Gainsborough, Romney, or Hopner served to remind him of the Shrimp Girl at Place, and of the little convalescent who resembled that famous picture.

In the evening he dined with two or three friends at the Carlton, and discussed the prospects of the approaching session, which were pronounced of the gloomiest. He walked back to his hotel through a wintry mist which just escaped being a fog, and he wished himself back in the clear brightness of the Cornish coast, where the Atlantic surges make solemn music all night long.

He had received no letter from Cornwall since he left; but he had no right to be surprised or offended at that. He had asked no one to write to him. He had not left Place till Moppet was pronounced out of danger; and he had given Danby full power to deal with the mother and her children. His plan was not to return to his house until after they had all left. He thought sometimes, almost with a shudder, how deadly quiet the rambling old house would seem when those young voices and those busy little feet should be heard in the corridors no more.

He bored himself in London for another day, and went to a small dinner-party in Grosvenor Square, where the talk was all of the session and where its prospects were pronounced of the brightest. Somebody remarked upon the pleasantness of town at this after-Christmas season, before the opening of Parliament had brought many people back, the only time in the London year when small snug dinners and general conversation were possible. Sir John remained mute, and thought that there could be no place more dismal than London in January.

It was nearly a week after he left Penlyon Place that he received the following telegram as he was dressing in the morning :—

"Moppet has asked for you very often, and has fretted at your absence, not without danger to her health. Pray come back.

"DANBY."

Danby again! A trick of Danby's to lure him back to his house and force on a reconciliation. He was vexed and angry with Danby; but he read that telegram twenty times over, making now very much, now very little of it; and he left London by the morning express from Waterloo, after telegraphing for his carriage to meet him at Launceston. In those days Launceston was the nearest station for Boscastle and Tintagel.

A long journey, throughout which—in spite of the mental occupation afforded by every newspaper that could be bought—his thoughts were haunted by the image of that sick child at Place, and could concentrate themselves on nothing else. The news of this wide busy world was nothing to him—foreign or domestic, rumours of war, earthquakes, cataclysms, a general upheaval, weighed as thistledown compared with the existence of one small child. She had asked for him, loving little creature; and he had not been there to respond to her tender yearning. Those little arms had been stretched out in vain. And she had been sorry—sorry even to sickness—a creature so delicate—so frail. He hated himself for the iron pride that had made him leave his house rather than brook the presence of his disobedient daughter.

It was after dark when he arrived at Place. Mr. Danby and Adela were in the hall to receive him when he alighted from his carriage. It was too late for any reasonable man to expect to see children about; yet he felt a pang of disappointment because there was no sound or sign of a child's presence.

"Well," he said fretfully, addressing himself to Danby, after bestowing an automatic kiss upon Adela, "your telegram has brought me back, you see. If the child wants to see me I am here to be seen; but no doubt she is fast asleep and happy—dreaming of her doll."

"I don't know that. It is the want of happy sleep that has told upon her. She was doing wonderfully well, the lungs getting quite sound again, and her strength picking up, when she began to fret at not seeing you. She was always asking to see you. Where was Sir John? Where was the kind old gentleman? Why wouldn't he come to see her? Was he angry with her for being ill? We explained that you were in London, would be back soon—but it was no use. However, I attached little importance to the matter. She was well cared for; she had her nearest and dearest. She would soon be strong enough to travel. We all talked to her cheerily of the return home. Children are so fond of change of any kind. It was only yesterday that I began to get anxious, and that Nicholls began to fear a brain attack. She had slept badly for two or three nights— had awakened, frightened and crying bitterly. Yesterday evening she became very feverish, and in the night she was delirious, and we were all uneasy about her. Hence my telegram. I hope I did not do wrong."

"You should have telegraphed sooner," said Sir John, warming his feet at the hall fire, with his back to Danby, "that's where you did wrong. I should like to see the child at once, if she is awake."

"I'll run and see," said Adela. "Mr. Nicholls went up to her room ten minutes ago, so I dare say she is awake."

" Is she so bad that Nicholls thinks it needful to see her in the evening ? " asked Sir John, gloomily.

" One cannot be too careful in such a case; and Nicholls is always careful. That child's brain is like touch-paper."

Adela came running downstairs. Moppet was wide awake and dying to see him, she told Sir John.

He waited for no further invitation, but hastened to that stately room where so many notable men and women of the West country had been entertained, and which was now occupied by a little figure which seemed absurdly small in the great carved four-post bed, an antique piece of furniture that looked like a Buddhist temple enshrining a very small idol under a tall and splendid canopy. The satin curtains of that ponderous four-poster had been embroidered by the women of the Penlyon family when homely Anne was queen.

There was a young woman sitting on the further side of Moppet's pillows, almost hidden by the curtain, and Mr. Nicholls was leaning against the tall, carved column at the foot of the bed, looking down at the little creature with the flushed face and over-bright eyes.

She turned her head at the opening of the door as quickly as a bird.

"Sir John! Sir John! Sir John!" she cried, clapping her feverish hands.

He was beside her in a moment. He leant over the bed—not even looking at the face on the other side— and clasped the tiny form to his breast.

"My darling!" he murmured, "my darling child!"

"Why did you go away just when I began to get well?" asked the innocent voice, so pure and true in its silver-sweet sound, that it seemed like the very spirit of truth itself, a something supersensuous and divine. "Why did you go away? I wanted you so badly."

"What, Moppet," he asked hoarsely, "when you had your mother?"

"Ah, but I wanted you too. I told you at Christmas I love you next to mother. And I wanted you very much, and it made me dream and cry in the night because you wasn't here."

"Ah, Sir John, you can't play any tune you like upon such fiddle-strings as those," said Nicholls, gravely.

BY HIS SIDE AS HE MADE HIS MORNING ROUND OF THE GARDENS
OR THE HOME FARM.

"My darling! my darling!"

That was almost as much as the old man could say. He sat down on the bed, and Moppet nestled into his waistcoat, as she used to do beside the library hearth, in the dusky hour before bedtime. She nestled there, and patted his strong hand with her tiny paw, and laughed and cried in a breath.

"Why did you go away?" she asked.

"God knows. Because I was a fool, perhaps."

"This is mother," said Moppet, plucking the curtain aside, and revealing a pale sweet face, with timid questioning eyes. "You don't know mother?"

Sir John stretched his hand across the bed, and the mother's hand clasped it, and the fair pale face bent down over it, and a daughter's lips kissed it again and again, fondly.

"Now you know mother," said Moppet. "You wouldn't have never known her if it hadn't been for me, but I didn't be ill on purpose, you know," explained Moppet.

No other word of peace or of forgiveness was ever

spoken between Sir John Penlyon and his only surviving child; but from that hour Sibyl Morland assumed her rightful position in her father's house. He was not a man who liked long speeches or fuss of any kind; and he took no pains to explain to his kindred or his friends how it was that the daughter who had been lost was found again; but assuredly that episode of the Christmas hirelings drew him and his old friend Danby nearer to each other than they had ever been yet, with a friendship that neither time nor circumstance could weaken.

Mrs. Morland took her place as a daughter in her father's house, but not the first place in her father's heart. That was occupied. Moppet had crept into the citadel by a postern gate, as it were, and reigned supreme there. Sir John's affection seemed to have skipped a generation, and the grandfather's love for his grandchild was warmer and deeper than ever the father's love had been. Moppet was his Benjamin, the child of his old age, who had come to him when life was dull and barren for lack of love.

Whoever might ostensibly govern at Penlyon Place, Moppet was the real master of the house, inasmuch as

SIR JOHN'S AFFECTION SEEMED TO HAVE SKIPPED A GENERATION.

R

she governed Sir John. Happily she was a beneficent ruler, full of sweet carefulness and tender thought for others, which increased with every year of her life. In all his walks and rides Moppet was Sir John's favourite companion, taking to her Shelty as a duckling to the farmyard pool, or trotting with little untiring feet by his side as he made his morning round of the gardens or the home farm. Before she had been three months at Place she knew the history, character, and capability of every horse in the stable; and she became a little wonder in her capacity for remembering and pronouncing the Greek or Latin names of tropical plants and flowers in the long range of hot-houses.

Laddie was despatched to an excellent preparatory school at Truro till such time as he should be old enough to go to Eton; and a governess was engaged to help Mrs. Morland in the care of her two little girls, such a dear old governess, warranted not to teach too much, and to see that they changed their shoes, being no other than that very Miss Peterson summarily dismissed by Mrs.

Hawberk, and whose dowdy figure moving quietly about the house and garden made Sir John Penlyon feel as if he were twenty years younger, by recalling the days when his motherless daughters were little children.

Visitors at Penlyon Place said that Lassie grew prettier every day, and that young lady's stately manners and graceful little airs were the subject of much admiration from casual observers, while Moppet's personality was disposed of off-hand as "interesting."

"I heard Lady St. Kew tell her husband that I was a plain likeness of the Shrimp Girl," she told her grandfather after an invasion of distinguished visitors. "*You* don't mind my being plain, do you?" she asked Sir John, her deep-set eyes searching his countenance.

"Mind? Why in my eyes you are the loveliest little woman in England."

Mrs. Hawberk, having made up her mind that her eldest daughter was to inherit a fortune as Sir John's only niece, was somewhat disappointed at the turn affairs had taken; but Adela's less worldly nature was incapable of any such unworthy feeling, and when her uncle helped to bring about her marriage with the man she loved by a gift of five thousand pounds she felt that she had every reason to be satisfied and grateful.

And what of bachelor Danby, without kindred or belongings in the world, drifting lightly down the river of life, like a withered leaf upon a forest stream? Who shall say that Mr. Danby has neither home nor home ties when they see the welcome that awaits his coming, the grief that attends his going, at Penlyon Place?

THE END.

LONDON :
PRINTED BY WILLIAM CLOWES AND SONS, LIMITED,
STAMFORD STREET AND CHARING CROSS.

MISS BRADDON'S NOVELS.

Ready at all Booksellers' and Bookstalls,
price **HALF A CROWN** each.

𝕿𝖍𝖊 𝕬𝖚𝖙𝖍𝖔𝖗'𝖘 𝕬𝖚𝖙𝖔𝖌𝖗𝖆𝖕𝖍 𝕰𝖉𝖎𝖙𝖎𝖔𝖓 of

MISS BRADDON'S NOVELS.

Also ready, price 2s. each, picture boards.

1. LADY AUDLEY'S SECRET.
2. HENRY DUNBAR.
3. ELEANOR'S VICTORY.
4. AURORA FLOYD.
5. JOHN MARCHMONT'S LEGACY.
6. THE DOCTOR'S WIFE.
7. ONLY A CLOD.
8. SIR JASPER'S TENANT.
9. TRAIL OF THE SERPENT.
10. LADY'S MILE.
11. LADY LISLE.
12. CAPTAIN OF THE "VULTURE."
13. BIRDS OF PREY.
14. CHARLOTTE'S INHERITANCE.
15. RUPERT GODWIN.
16. RUN TO EARTH.
17. DEAD SEA FRUIT.
18. RALPH THE BAILIFF.
19. FENTON'S QUEST.
20. LOVELS OF ARDEN.
21. ROBERT AINSLEIGH.
22. TO THE BITTER END.
23. MILLY DARRELL.
24. STRANGERS AND PILGRIMS.
25. LUCIUS DAVOREN.
26. TAKEN AT THE FLOOD.
27. LOST FOR LOVE.
28. A STRANGE WORLD.
29. HOSTAGES TO FORTUNE.
30. DEAD MEN'S SHOES.
31. JOSHUA HAGGARD.
32. WEAVERS AND WEFT.
33. AN OPEN VERDICT.
34. VIXEN.
35. THE CLOVEN FOOT.
36. THE STORY OF BARBARA.
37. JUST AS I AM.
38. ASPHODEL.
39. MOUNT ROYAL.
40. THE GOLDEN CALF.
41. PHANTOM FORTUNE.
42. FLOWER AND WEED.
43. ISHMAEL.
44. WYLLARD'S WEIRD.
45. UNDER THE RED FLAG.
46. ONE THING NEEDFUL.
47. MOHAWKS.
48. LIKE AND UNLIKE.
49. THE FATAL THREE.
50. THE DAY WILL COME.
51. ONE LIFE ONE LOVE.
52. GERARD.
53. THE VENETIANS.
54. ALL ALONG THE RIVER.
55. THOU ART THE MAN.

[In due course.

LONDON: SIMPKIN, MARSHALL, HAMILTON, KENT & CO., LTD.

A SELECT LIST OF RECENT PUBLICATIONS.

London, E.C. : Simpkin, Marshall, Hamilton, Kent & Co., Ltd.

WELCOME GIFT-BOOKS FOR YOUNG OR OLD,

And Delightful Companions for a Country Ramble.

With over 1000 Examples in Colours and Outline.
Crown 8vo   Cloth, 6s.; leather, 10s.

OUR COUNTRY'S FLOWERS, and How to Know Them. Being a Complete Guide to the Flowers and Ferns of Britain. By W. J. GORDON. With an Introduction by Rev. GEORGE HENSLOW, M.A., F.L.S., F.G.S.

With Illustrations in Colours of every Species.
Crown 8vo.   Cloth, 6s.; leather, 10s.

OUR COUNTRY'S BIRDS, and How to Know Them. A Guide to all the Birds of Great Britain. By W. J. GORDON. With many original Diagrams.

INDISPENSABLE TO EVERY LOVER OF NATURE.

These two books have been produced uniform in style and binding, and will be found thoroughly reliable and practical.

Also in preparation, uniform in style and price.

OUR COUNTRY'S BUTTERFLIES AND MOTHS.

SIMPKIN, MARSHALL, HAMILTON, KENT & CO., LTD.

HANDSOMELY ILLUSTRATED GIFT-BOOKS.

Royal 4to. £1 5s.

THE SCHOOL FOR SCANDAL. A Comedy.

By RICHARD BRINSLEY SHERIDAN.

With exquisitely Coloured Illustrations scattered throughout the text, and dainty miniatures of the Dramatis Personæ on choice cloth cover.

Imperial 4to.   Quarter morocco, gilt edges, each leaf mounted on linen guard. £1 11s. 6d.

OTHELLO: THE MOOR OF VENICE. A Tragedy.

By WILLIAM SHAKESPEARE.

With facsimile reproductions of Twenty Water-colour Drawings by L. MARCHETTI, and numerous Engravings.

Imperial 4to. £1 5s.

ROMEO AND JULIET. A Tragedy.

By WILLIAM SHAKESPEARE.

With beautifully Coloured and other Illustrations by MARCHETTI, ROSSI, and CORTAZZO.

SIMPKIN, MARSHALL, HAMILTON, KENT & CO., LTD.

"Very interesting for those who care for old houses and old families"
—TIMES.

Oblong 8vo.   15s.

MANNINGTON AND THE WALPOLES, EARLS OF ORFORD.

By LADY DOROTHY NEVILL.

With Fifty Illustrations.   *Royal 4to.*   15s.

THE BARBIZON SCHOOL OF PAINTERS.—1.
COROT.

By DAVID CROAL THOMPSON,

Author of "The Life of Thomas Bewick," "The Life of Phiz," etc.

New and Enlarged Edition, with 156 Illustrations.   *8vo.*   12s.

JAPAN AND ITS ART.

By MARCUS B. HUISH.

Works by Leighton, Millais, Mason, Waterhouse, Marcus Stone, Whistler, Holman Hunt, Burne-Jones, Romney, Rossetti, etc.

Folio, £2 2s. net.   Large Paper Edition, £4 4s. net.

MASTERPIECES OF ART.

Forty Reproductions of Pictures in the Guildhall Loan Exhibition, 1894.

SIMPKIN, MARSHALL, HAMILTON, KENT & CO., LTD.

THREE NEW BOOKS.

Small 4to.   Cloth, 8s. net.

CATHERINE HUTTON AND HER FRIENDS.

By Mrs. CATHERINE HUTTON BEALE,

Author of " The Reminiscences of a Gentlewoman of the Last Century."

All who like a picture of the manners and society of the eighteenth century, and those who care to linger among the byways of that fascinating time, will welcome Mrs. Beale's " Catherine Hutton and her Friends."

Square crown 8vo.   3s. 6d.

FAIRBRASS: A Child's Story.

By T. EDGAR PEMBERTON.

With Illustrations by KATE E. BUNCE.

Mr. Pemberton has given us some quaint sketches full of humour and pathos and touching episodes. The book is admirably got up and well illustrated.

Fcap. 4to.   3s. 6d.

GOOD KING WENCESLAS:

A Carol Decorated and Pictured by ARTHUR J. GASKIN.
With an Introduction by WILLIAM MORRIS.

Also a **Special** **Edition** *(limited to 113 Copies), printed on Arnold's unbleached hand-made paper.* 25s *net.*

SIMPKIN, MARSHALL, HAMILTON, KENT & CO., LTD.

Second Edition. Demy 8vo 474 pages. Cloth. Price 7s 6d.

HADDEN'S HANDBOOK ON THE LOCAL GOVERNMENT ACT, 1894.

Being a Complete and Practical Guide to the above Act and its Incorporated Enactments.

To which are appended the Full Text of the Act, the Incorporated Sections of the Local Government Act, 1888, The Ballot Act, 1872, The Public Health Act, 1875, The Municipal Corporations Act, 1882; The Municipal Elections (Corrupt and Illegal Practices) Act, 1884; The Allotments Act, 1887 and 1890, and of other Statutes; together with the Circulars and Orders issued by the Local Government Board, and other Official Information.

SHORT STALKS;

OR,

HUNTING CAMPS, NORTH, SOUTH, EAST, and WEST.

By EDWARD NORTH BUXTON.

With numerous Illustrations by LODGE, WHYMPER, WOLF, and others

Printed by R. & R. CLARK, and bound in buckram. 8vo. 21s

Crown 8vo. Cloth Boards, 2s. 6d, post free

CLUBS: ATHLETIC AND RECREATIVE.

HINTS AS TO THEIR FORMATION AND MANAGEMENT, INCLUDING TECHNICAL SUGGESTIONS AS TO THE LEGAL POSITION AND LIABILITY OF OFFICERS, AND THE RECOVERY OF SUBSCRIPTIONS

By KARSLAKE DENE, Solicitor.

CONTENTS.—Introductory—Chap. I —The Preliminary Meeting. II —The Adjourned Meeting III —The Chairman. IV.—The Committee and Bye-Laws, etc. V —The Secretary. VI.—The Treasurer. VII —Club Property and Winding-up Rules. VIII —Election of Members IX —Expulsion of Members. X.—Duties of Members. XI.—Annual and Special Meetings. XII —Miscellaneous Appendix of Forms

With many Illustrative Notes from Unpublished Letters. 2 vols. About 900 pages. Demy 8vo. Price 32s

THE FAMILIAR LETTERS OF SIR WALTER SCOTT.

FROM THE ORIGINALS AT ABBOTSFORD AND ELSEWHERE.

SIMPKIN, MARSHALL, HAMILTON, KENT & CO, LTD.

THE STORY OF THE PHŒNIX PARK MURDERS.

THE WORKING OF THE PARNELL-FENIAN ALLIANCE.

THE SECRET HISTORY OF THE ASSASSINATIONS
IN DUBLIN, 1882.

Demy 8vo, 640 pages, with Eight Portraits   One Guinea.

THE IRISH NATIONAL INVINCIBLES AND THEIR TIMES.

By PATRICK J P. TYNAN ("Number One").

Demy 8vo, 16 pp.   Sixpence.

"NUMBER ONE'S BOOK."

By Ed. Caulfield Houston.

The *Westminster Gazette's* Admission—The Worth of Tynan's State-
ments—The Dublin Star Chamber Inquiry and its Outcome—The *Times*
and the Letters—The Special Commission and the League Funds—The
Secrets of Dublin Castle—The Redmondite Organ Corroborates !

Popular Edition.   Crown 8vo.   Boards, 2s. 6d.,; cloth, 3s. 6d.

TWENTY-FIVE YEARS IN THE SECRET SERVICE: The Recollections of a Spy.

By Major Henri Le Caron.

The Library Edition, with Portrait and Facsimiles, 8vo, cloth, price 14s.,
is still on sale.
Also a few copies of the First Edition, 8vo, price 21s. net.

Fifth Edition.   8vo. 3s. net.

THE CAMPAIGN GUIDE: An Election Handbook for Unionist Speakers.

In Four Parts.   Part 1: Conservative and Unionist Work.   Part 2:
Ireland.   Part 3: Gladstonian Government, 1892-4.   Part 4: Election
Problems.

SIMPKIN, MARSHALL, HAMILTON, KENT & CO., Ltd.

In Two Volumes. Demy 4to Antique. Price £6 6s. net.

THE HISTORY OF "WHITE'S:"

With the Betting Book from 1743 to 1878,

AND

A List of Members from 1736 to 1892.

With Two Hundred Full-page Illustrations, chiefly Portraits in Collotype.

In Two Volumes, pp. 785 and 745. 8vo. Cloth. £1 10s.

A NEW DICTIONARY OF THE PORTUGUESE AND ENGLISH LANGUAGES.

ENRICHED BY A GREAT NUMBER OF TECHNICAL TERMS USED IN COMMERCE AND INDUSTRY, IN THE ARTS AND SCIENCES, AND INCLUDING A GREAT VARIETY OF EXPRESSIONS FROM THE LANGUAGE OF DAILY LIFE

BASED ON A MANUSCRIPT OF JULIUS CORNET.

By H. MICHAELIS.

IN TWO VOLUMES.

VOLUME I.	VOLUME II.
PORTUGUESE-ENGLISH.	ENGLISH-PORTUGUESE.

SIMPKIN, MARSHALL, HAMILTON, KENT & CO, Ltd

WORKS AT 6s.

THE EBB-TIDE: A Trio and Quartette.

By Robert Louis Stevenson and Lloyd Osbourne.

HEROES IN HOMESPUN: Scenes and Stories from the American Emancipation Movement.

By Ascott R. Hope.

With Portraits, Illustrations, and Maps. 4to.

THE DOWNFALL OF LOBENGULA: The Cause, History, and Effect of the Matabeli War.

By W. A. Wills and L. T. Collingridge.

With Contributions by Major P. W. Forbes, Major Sir J. C. Willoughby, Mr. H. Rider Haggard, Mr F. C. Selous, F.Z S, and Mr. P. B. S. Wrey, A M Inst.C.E.

Royal 8vo 6s.

BALANCING FOR EXPERT BOOK-KEEPERS.

By George Pepler Norton, F.C.A.,

Author of "Textile Manufacturers' Book-Keeping," etc.; Prizeman, Final Examination of the Institute of Chartered Accountants, 1883

4to.   7s. 6d.

SHORT METHOD EX-MERIDIAN TABLES.

Computed for intervals of One Minute between the Parallels of Latitude 0° and 60° inclusive, with Instructions for Using the Tables in French, German, Spanish, Portuguese, Italian, Dutch, and Scandinavian.

By John F. R. Bateman, Lieutenant R.N., And Assistants.

SIMPKIN, MARSHALL, HAMILTON, KENT & CO., Ltd.